T0356293

Praise for *Why the World Doesn't Make Sense*

"A powerful wake-up call for those trying to understand our chaotic world, Menedis expertly unravels the intricate web of global control and guides us back to personal sovereignty."

— UngaTheGreat, Data Scientist and Citizen Journalist

"In an era fraught with heightened uncertainty over AI, cyber-attacks, hot wars, political polarization, escalating geopolitical tensions, and massive economic disruption it is hard for anyone to make sense of the world. Christine Menedis's book *Why the World Doesn't Make Sense* is a rare and welcome surprise that offers clear signal through all the noise. She not only helps the reader understand how we got here but, more importantly, provides a way to navigate a path forward. In a time when most people feel helpless to effect change, Menedis reminds us we each have agency in our lives and can make a difference. This is refreshing and hopeful. Her book offers a rare combination of knowledge and wisdom and should be essential reading—not just for academics and business and political leaders, but for citizens of all walks of life."

— Paul H. Stebbins, Chairman Emeritus,
   World Kinect Corporation

"*Why the World Doesn't Make Sense* isn't just a starting point—it's a companion for anyone serious about navigating the evolving world of money, bitcoin, and digital assets. This is more than a book; it's a guide for sovereign individuals ready to take control of their future."

— Victor H. Herrera, VP and Managing Director,
   Rolex Boutique Luxury Swiss

"A powerful wake-up call! This book challenges the forces that threaten our well-being and personal sovereignty. Christine delivers an essential and eye-opening read—be aware, be all-in!"

— Vlad Kapustin, Managing Member, Interkap Group

"Ms. Menedis takes the reader on a fascinating journey beginning with Socratic thought and weaving its way via the rediscovery of the nature of democracy, the intent of the Founding Fathers, capitalism, liberalism, autocracy, fascism, ethics, and the occult. Her book delves deeply into the differences between individual and collective sovereignty using metaphors involving subjects as varied as digital currencies, media disinformation, and even the control wielded by global cartels."

—Bharat Bhise, CEO, Bravia Capital

"There are some books where you glean an idea and others where everything is an idea. This remarkable book is the latter. Whether you agree with the contents is immaterial—these are ideas to be wrestled with. A must-read."

—Thomas E. McGlynn, Chairman of the
Board, SanAir Technologies Laboratory

"Prepare to have your assumptions upended. In *Why the World Doesn't Make Sense*, Menedis dismantles the familiar narratives that keep us complacent and challenges us to think differently. With unflinching clarity and practical wisdom, this book will push you out of your comfort zone and into the driver's seat of your own destiny."

—Stephen Alex, MD, Orthopaedic, Hand,
and Microvascular Surgeon

"It's time to dig deep and more closely examine the economic, social, digital, and political forces that impact our day-to-day lives and, more importantly, that will impact our future generations. This book can kick-start that conversation. *Why the World Doesn't Make Sense* is an insightful must-read no matter where you fall on the ideological spectrum."

—Shirin Toor, Chief of Staff to Global Chief
Transformation Officer at PWC

"*Why the World Doesn't Make Sense* is a question on everyone's mind, and Menedis answers it with wisdom, clarity, and a much-needed dose of hope. By steering us back to first-principles thinking, this book reminds us that even in uncertainty, we have the power to understand, to act, and to shape a future we believe in."

—Ken Bakshi, Managing Partner, Trishul Capital

"*Why the World Doesn't Make Sense* is a must-read! Menedis fearlessly tackles the chaos of our times, challenging complacency and inspiring action. Each chapter is filled with powerful insights that ignite a fire within you. If you're ready to break free from the ordinary and embrace your greatness, grab this book and start your transformation today!"

—Maritza Cuellar, International Real Estate Broker

"Christine's sharp insights and bold perspective make this book an essential read for anyone seeking clarity in an increasingly complex world. She delivers a thought-provoking and empowering narrative that challenges conventional thinking."

—Sanjay Aggarwal, Cofounder and Managing Director,
SAR Trilogy Management; Honorary Consul,
Consulate of St. Kitts and Nevis in Miami

"Christine and I have connected on many levels—regulation, politics, crypto, and as people—and it's amazing to see how she's brought her perspectives together into one cohesive and insightful read!"

—Jacob Martin, General Partner, 2 Punks Capital

"*Why the World Doesn't Make Sense* is a thought-provoking examination of the subtle forces eroding personal freedom in contemporary society. This book serves both as a wake-up call and a guide for those of us who feel disoriented in a world rife with contradictions. Menedis encourages readers to reclaim their independence, question centralized authority, and defend their personal liberties in an era marked by unprecedented global influence. For those interested in exploring the intricate dynamics between individual freedom and societal structures, *Why the World Doesn't Make Sense* promises to be an enlightening and empowering read."

—Rob Graifman, Founder, Thylacine Capital LLC

Why the World Doesn't Make Sense

Why the World Doesn't Make Sense

RECLAIMING THE
LIBERTY YOU DIDN'T KNOW
YOU LOST

BY CHRISTINE MENEDIS

Forefront
B O O K S

Published by Forefront Books, Nashville, Tennessee.
Distributed by Simon & Schuster.

Library of Congress Control Number: 2024926958

Print ISBN: 978-1-63763-431-8
E-book ISBN: 978-1-63763-432-5

Cover Design by Bruce Gore, Gore Studio, Inc.
Interior Design by PerfecType, Nashville, TN

Printed in the United States of America

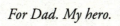

For Dad. My hero.

CONTENTS

INTRODUCTION | BEFORE YOU BEGIN

If you do not change direction, you may end up where you are heading.

—Lao Tzu

The world is at a crucible moment. It's palpable. Something is about to break. Millions of people across the globe *want* something to break.

You might be one of them. Frustrated. Angry. Confused. Wondering what happened to your country, your community, perhaps even yourself.

The unholy trio of globalist organizations, governments, and large corporations is aggressively snuffing out non-compliant voices, while somehow normalizing an agenda that would have seemed intolerable to the vast majority of people everywhere mere decades ago.

The now-apparent child of a bioweapons program gone wrong, COVID-19 changed our relationships with each other and with our constitutions. Censorship. Surveillance. Authoritarianism. They're back. On steroids.

Humanity is facing issues impacting our health, our food supply, our energy, and our connection to our land, not to mention an obvious loss of all basic freedoms. But can we talk about it in public? Hard no.

We're taught that everyone has the power to determine their own "truth." And yet, simultaneously, no one can be trusted to digest unapproved information and form their own opinions, never mind repeat them to others. God forbid.

No, we live in the age of information terrorism, where mis-, dis-, and malinformation (referred to as MDM) have been "conveniently" classified by the US Department of Homeland Security as three new forms of terrorism and earning those who peddle them the classification of "domestic threat actors."[1]

Incidentally, malinformation is defined as true, as something that is "based in fact," just not used in an approved manner. It's here that the lawyer in me feels the need to make you aware that *terrorism* isn't just a turn of phrase used for dramatic effect. It's a legal term of art[2] and means that the constitutional protection of your rights is no longer guaranteed. And within this context, it has one and only one purpose: to have a chilling effect on free speech.

With the mainstream media so clearly passé, ours is now the era of independent citizen journalists. The era of independent media. And dissent in the form of independent media is, of course, the most dangerous of all. Independent media inevitably leads to independent thought. And that, above all else, simply cannot be tolerated.

To control thought and speech is, by definition, totalitarian. But where is this coming from? And why so many willing participants? How has this culture evidencing a seeming disdain and hatred for humanity become so commonplace?

At a time when the world is undeniably witnessing the greatest prosperity in its history, why do we see an intentional effort by those at the helm to take two steps back for every one we've taken forward? Greed and a lust for power can only explain so much. Some have proffered that perhaps it's an innate and subconscious human reflex when we don't feel our success was properly earned. A perverse impulse that causes our leaders to self-destruct at a national and international level in the same way so many of us do in our own daily lives. Perhaps it's just an irresistible, if tragic, human impulse to burn things down upon achieving them.

Others, as we'll see, have proffered that it's something deep-seated. Intentional. Ideological. An extreme form of liberalism run amok.

The problems of our "polycrisis" are well documented and articulated by authors and commentators across the Western world. What we don't see are a lot of are viable solutions. Actionable solutions.

Despite what our politicians tell us, we can't vote our way out of this mess. Election victories bring hope, but no guarantees.

Nor can we simply be distracted by war, even the "right" war, and shoot our way out. The reality is that we can't even move to a small town, turn off the TV, and ignore it. We'd still be subject to the rules, regulations, and monetary theft everyone else is. Though, perhaps we'd be a little happier. At least until the rest of society's ills reached our hamlet.

No. If we're going to reclaim our societies, our discourse, and our nations, we must first lay claim to ourselves. We must embrace our sovereign nature, as individuals capable of recognizing and throwing off the yoke of secular collectivism in all its forms, so that we can live engaging, satisfying, and successful lives wherever we are. We must lay claim to the pursuit of happiness. Of course, doing so requires overcoming our anger and frustration and removing ourselves from the loop of technology-enhanced outrage.

Anger often arises from feelings of weakness, whether due to a lack of control or a lack of understanding. Far too many freedom-loving people feel impotent in today's world, believing they're unable to change their situation and achieve their desired outcome. Luckily, the fix is simple: knowledge. After all, knowledge is power.

Knowledge provides us with the tools and information we need to take effective action. And it eliminates our impotence, restoring our power, because it equips us to influence outcomes more effectively. When we understand a situation or concept, it demystifies it for us, which in turn, reduces our feelings of frustration and puts us back in control.

Through our God-given reason and intellect, we're meant to grapple with the truth and revelation of all created things; therefore, it's essential that we understand all parts of our society, including politics, money, and the ideas that drive them. We may not be of this world, but we are here in it, and the decisions we make—and the actions we take—matter.

We seek secular knowledge and wisdom in order to make the most of our time here on this beautiful Earth and out of a quest for truth and a love for our neighbors. But we must ultimately fix our gaze on the eternal.

As we move forward together, I will do more than simply explain the ideas shaping today's world—I'm going to name them. I'm calling them what they are. You see, naming something is a powerful act; it gives us a way to understand, categorize, and manage things. When we name a concept, we bring it into sharp focus, and it is no longer something ambiguous or overwhelming but specific and definable. Naming things helps us understand what we're dealing with.

Naming something also gives us a sense of control over it. When we identify and label an issue, we can start to address it directly. It's no longer an uncontrollable and abstract problem; now it's something tangible that we can interact with.

Naming further allows us to communicate our experiences to others and share more effectively. This leads to enhanced support and collaboration—a requisite if we're going to change our world for the better.

Finally, naming is empowering. It gives us dominion over the concepts that are now within our understanding and control. It's no accident that in the book of Genesis God had man name the wild animals and all other living creatures.

Or that in Orthodox Christian baptism, we are given a name by which God knows and calls us. Words matter. It's a concept we'll return to time and again in these pages.

Today's world is a complicated place, full of friends, enemies, and even frenemies. Nothing is black and white. Truly understanding it requires holding multiple competing ideas in your head at the same time. Having the same enemy doesn't mean you're driving toward the same outcome. Far from it.

I sense an extreme urgency to stress the importance of all this because, sadly, the world looks to be gearing up for trouble. It's just that point in history. We're due. While campaigning for reelection, President Donald Trump narrowly survived an assassination attempt. The gunman's bullet tore through his ear rather than his skull. He later stated it was only by the grace of God that he survived. And one can't help but agree with him. But with a country on the brink of chaos, what if he hadn't? What would America—the world, for that matter—have looked like the day after?

Don't allow yourself to become a pawn in a fight that you don't understand. For far too long, we've left philosophy to the academics and allowed our young to be trained rather than taught. That stops now. By the time you reach the end of this book, I believe that you will be able to identify, name, and understand the major themes of our times. And I ask that when you close it for the last time, you hand it to someone whom you think could benefit from this knowledge.

What you think and agree with, and where you decide to go from here, is completely up to you. You are a free individual. *You* are sovereign.

Throughout this book, we'll turn to the concept of sovereignty. What is it? What makes one a sovereign individual? And why talk about personal sovereignty at all? Isn't freedom enough?

Fascinatingly, a basic Google search today classifies sovereignty as a term to be applied to nations or clans of people with political self-determination, rather than to individuals. This conspicuous removal of the entire concept of personal sovereignty is telling.

The recognition of the individual as sovereign is *the* great discovery of Western civilization. From it sprang truths that were eventually understood by mankind to be "self-evident." Yet today, entire generations have lost this understanding. Can you answer these simple questions: Why are the truths articulated in America's Declaration of Independence self-evident? And do we even still recognize them that way?

While freedom typically refers to the absence of external constraints, personal sovereignty goes further, in that it emphasizes the additional importance of self-mastery and responsibility. It also emphasizes the conscious exercise of one's power to make values-aligned choices, rather than being swayed by societal expectations or external pressures. Radio legend Paul Harvey used to refer to this as the freedom to do what you should. I love that idea.

Sovereignty is simultaneously an ideal to strive for and a practical approach to living in a world with complex social and political structures. It works because it is man embracing his true, God-given nature.

Most importantly, sovereignty can be your personal solution to what today's chaos erupts into. And get enough sovereign individuals together . . . well, you have yourself a free society. The type that was envisioned in America's founding documents yet, to this day, has not fully played out in reality.

This book is meant to be pondered. Go outside. Take a walk. Touch nature as you mull over these ideas.

We begin with a few foundational chapters about truth, money, and natural law—requisite armament for any freedom-loving sovereign individual.

Governance structures change, and the current nation state will likely not last forever. But that's neither here nor there in the bigger picture. What must be secured so that it can endure is the understanding and recognition of our sovereign nature, our inherent God-given rights. In the words of American revolutionary Thomas Paine: "Man did not enter into society to become worse than he was before, nor to have fewer rights than he had before, but to have those rights better secured. His natural rights are the foundation of all his civil rights."[3]

Why is money listed as a requisite armament? Simple. Money is the principal weapon used to *create* poverty and dependency, not eradicate them. Without an adequate understanding of financial principles, there can be no sovereignty. Societal evils are allowed to continue to occur because naive people fail to grasp money's principal role as a weapon. And, as with any weapon, we can be on either side of it.

James Madison, American revolutionary and US president, taught us that the advancement and diffusion of knowledge is the only guardian of true liberty.[4] Hence, the emphasis throughout this book is on arming you not only with knowledge but with the tools to continue to grow and expand on that knowledge as well.

'Cause here's the thing: Everyone loves a blank slate. But we're fresh out of land. There's no place left to go. We're going to have to figure this thing out. Together.

CHAPTER ONE | **TRUTH**

In a time of deceit, telling the truth is a revolutionary act.

—George Orwell

PERSONAL SOVEREIGNTY | WHAT IS IT, REALLY?

Personal sovereignty. It's the simple idea that an individual possesses the right to full self-ownership and self-determination, that they are free from external control and coercion. Think individual liberty and autonomy (having the freedom to govern yourself and your affairs). Critically, sovereign individuals (those who actively embrace their true nature) also have the *ability* to do so.

The practical aspects of personal sovereignty are important to understand because we may just be coming to a place and a time where we have to opt out of "the system" in order to preserve our beliefs, to preserve our soul. Will you have that ability?

If—and when—the wheels fall off, you don't want to be sick, weak, or dependent on others. You want to be strong and independent. Self-sufficient. Self-sovereign.

Life, Liberty, and the Pursuit of Happiness

Sovereign individuals are eager to champion causes that promote freedom—whether pertaining to Life (food, energy, health), Liberty (money, transacting, speech, privacy), or the Pursuit of Happiness (property, integrity).

Sovereign. Let's examine this word.

When some people hear the words "sovereign individual," they might think "prepper," someone manning their nuclear bunker that's stocked with food-filled glass jars (or worse, buckets of dehydrated foods) and boxes upon boxes of ammunition. Not that there's anything wrong with that . . .

But the reality is that you can embrace these practical aspects of sovereignty anywhere. While preppers offer an extreme example, what's really being discussed is *preparedness*—with or without a bunker full of dried beans. But this is not a bad thing. As sovereign individuals, we must be prepared in mind, body, and soul for whatever life throws our way. This includes our homes, our finances, our basic needs. In short, we must be prepared for grey rhinos.

Life is filled with animal analogies—from the "canary in the coalmine" (an early warning of a potential hazard) to a "red herring" (strategically placed information to mislead and distract from actual threats) to a "black swan" event (an unforeseeable event with significant effects on international and domestic politics). But let's focus on this "black swan." Warnings by current thought leaders about an imminent black swan event have almost become in vogue. However, their warnings actually reflect their own confusion about the term. You see, the definition states that it is an *unforeseeable* event. So to warn us about an imminent but unforeseeable situation is a contradiction. What they are really warning us to plan for are the "grey rhinos," the obvious risks that we acknowledge but tend to ignore. They are underestimated risks. Somewhere in the back of our minds, we know they're there, but the likelihood of our experiencing them seems so low to us that it's just easier for us to ignore them.

Of course, this doesn't make them any less impactful. Classic examples of grey rhinos are 9/11, COVID-19, and the October 7 attack on Israel by Hamas terrorists. They are well-known, world-altering threats, but ones that we ignored for too long. As I write this, the rhinos on the horizon include the de-dollarization of the world economy, food shortages, cyber events, and an unfreezing of conflicts on the Korean peninsula. We must have plans in place for all of them.

As pointed out by journalist Benedikt Franke, "Much of the popularity of the black swan is down to yet another animal analogy, namely 'the elephant in the room.' This refers to pressing, often uncomfortable matters that we choose to avoid in the hope of escaping their consequences. The aversion to confronting things head-on makes the black swan an attractive concept for those who would like to pretend that there was no way of seeing a particular challenge coming."[5]

Sovereign individuals know that most black swans are really grey rhinos. We are not taken by surprise.

While asserting our own independence, we must also respect the rights and freedoms of our fellow man, acknowledging that each of us has the same right to self-sovereignty.

Critically, with freedom comes responsibility. While we often strive for a degree of self-reliance and independence from overly controlling systems, institutions, and governments, as sovereign individuals, we are willingly accountable for our own actions and their subsequent consequences. No nanny states here.

This is not simply a "live and let live" mentality. We who embrace our true sovereign nature understand that this freedom and this love for our fellow man is far more profound, and that our responsibility extends far beyond the mere civic spectrum. Fundamental to the once self-evident truths of Western civilization is that we are endowed with certain rights from our Creator because we are made in His image and possess the power to bring order to chaos with our consciousness and our reason.

From its first words, the book of Genesis posits that if you act in truth, then the order you produce is good, regardless of how it appears to others. It's an axiomatic ethical proposition. In short, truth matters. It's why the twisting of truth we see all around us is so dark, and why we as sovereign individuals have a duty to use our logos (words, truth, speech) and our reason to create order out of the current chaos, to do good.[6] Psychologist Jordan Peterson, who has written and lectured extensively on these topics, has insightfully pointed out that this makes us cocreators of reality. For thousands of years, Orthodox Christians have agreed with this view, that mankind acts as cocreators with the Uncreated Maker. Thus, man has the task—and the opportunity—to reflect God in His creation.

It's hard to imagine a greater responsibility (or opportunity) accompanying the gift of our sovereignty.

Logos

Logos is a concept with deep philosophical and theological significance, rooted in ancient Greek philosophy and Christianity.

In secular philosophy, you can think of (capital L) *Logos* as the principle of order, reason, and meaning that brings structure to the universe—as divine reason or the fundamental structure that underpins existence.

In Christianity, *Logos* (capital L) refers to Jesus Christ, the eternal Word of God. In the Bible, the Gospel of John describes Logos as being with God from the beginning and as the source of all creation: "In the beginning was the Word [Logos], and the Word was with God, and the Word was God" (John 1:1).

In Christian thought, *logoi* (lowercase l) are the divine principles or purposes embedded by God in all of creation. Everything in the universe has a *logos* that reflects His wisdom and plan; *logoi* connect creation to the eternal *Logos* and give everything meaning and purpose. Humans are created in God's image and are meant to understand and live in harmony with these *logoi*. By doing so, we can grow spiritually and move closer to God. This journey is about recognizing God's presence in all things and becoming more united with Christ.

Both the Church and secular philosophy understand (lowercase l) *logos* as human reason, intellect, and capacity for speech and truth. In Christianity, these are seen as gifts from God that reflect the divine *Logos*. Reason can help us understand the created world, while words and intellect are meant to communicate and seek truth in harmony with God's wisdom. In short, speaking truthfully has the power to constructively shape reality. We are meant to seek and speak truth.

See further John 1:1–14.

THREE REQUIREMENTS TO ACT | ARE WE THERE YET?

America was instituted on a simple, but powerful idea: The individual is the one who gets to make the ultimate decisions surrounding their own life. Not the collective. Yet today, "We the People" somehow no longer care about this great gift that history bestowed on us. Few among us still understand it in our core.

American self-sovereignty in its purest form is an understanding that our rights come from God—intrinsic to us, inseparable from who we are.[7] But we get busy and, frankly, have other things to do, so we implement a government of other men to protect our rights. And the moment that government is no longer serving us by protecting those God-given rights, it isn't just our right—it's our *duty* to overthrow that government.

I recognize that this simple eternal truth sounds heretical in this day and age. And that's why we're rapidly surrendering our personal and property rights. Our money. Our land. Our food. Our shelter. Media personality Tucker Carlson has sagely pointed out that no one is willing to die for anything anymore. And it's true. As you look at the world around you, what principles would you be willing to take a last stand for? Do you even believe you have the right to do so anymore? The obvious has somehow become the unthinkable, the undoable.

Freedom is in our blood. William Pitt the Elder was a British statesman and prime minister in the 1700s. Seeking to explain to his colleagues in the House of Lords what motivated the rebellious American colonists, Pitt described a people "who prefer Poverty with Liberty, to Golden Chains and Sordid Affluence; and who will die in defense of their Rights, as Men—as Freemen."[8] Could that still be said of us today?

Advances in technology have brought innumerable benefits to mankind—lifting billions out of abject poverty. Yet, at the same time, we have allowed ourselves to become enslaved by our own creations—mesmerized by the afforded convenience. Why leave your house when an app allows you to order delivery online? Why talk to a girl when all you have to do is swipe right? Why go to the office when you can just Zoom? Why seek knowledge when you can always just ask Google or ChatGPT? Why read and contemplate the words when you can simply listen while multitasking? Why stand up for your rights when things are just so darn convenient? Sure, you're getting screwed left, right, and center. But life is easy, so get over it.

"Golden Chains and Sordid Affluence." America—and much of the Western world—has a comfort problem.

Perhaps you don't fall into the convenience trap, and you do long for liberty. Perhaps yours is instead a fear trap. Fear you'll be scorned and mocked by society, made to look like a radical or, worse, a naive fool. Fear of your perceived powerlessness being exposed as reality. As part of a society no longer faithful to God nor strengthened and emboldened by our close connection to Him, perhaps you simply don't believe that a better state can be achieved. At least not by you or anyone you know.

Austrian School economist Ludwig von Mises noted three requirements for humans to act: (1) dissatisfaction with the present state of affairs, (2) a vision of a better state, and (3) the belief that we can reach that better state.[9] When just one of these requirements is missing, people will not act.

Obviously, this is not an America-only problem; there is worldwide dissatisfaction with the present state of affairs and the heightened control we are living under. And while it could be argued that the vision of a better state is lacking, the guiding principles are well articulated and shared by many. There can be no question that people across the globe envision a free society—one where "community" isn't code for socialism or submission. But rather, it's the voluntary coming together of strong, sovereign individuals. This leaves the belief that we can reach that better state. Whether due to technological enslavement via convenience, distancing from God, lack of knowledge and/or historical context, or general downtroddenment, this absence of belief that we can reach that better state is clearly the problem.

After all, why die for something you don't believe is winnable? Why even try to stand up? We have lost faith in our God, our families, and ourselves. Far removed from our rich history of rebels and revolutionaries, we have allowed ourselves to become weak in mind, body, and spirit.

As Michael Hopf so aptly stated: "Hard times create strong men. Strong men create good times. Good times create weak men. And, weak men create hard times."[10] Hard times are about to be upon us, my friends.

EMBRACING TRUTH | BUILDING A FOUNDATION

Today's society spends an inordinate amount of time arguing about symptoms rather than identifying and dealing with root causes. And it makes sense. They're what we see, what's directly impacting our lives. Not to mention, symptoms are far easier to deal with. Untangling a vast bureaucratic administrative state seems impossible, but surely, we can deal with inflation or stop the funding of the latest war that should have never started. And so, society plays whack-a-mole as these symptoms inevitably continue to pop up across all spectrums of our lives.

Since the dawn of humanity, man has wrestled with its desire for power and control. It wasn't enough to have dominion over nature. We wanted it over each other. The cycles of history can often be distilled down to eras of control versus freedom or, as many think of it today, eras of centralization versus decentralization.

America and many countries around the world are currently experiencing waves of populism—defined as an approach that strives to appeal to ordinary people who feel their concerns are disregarded by established power-entrenched groups (often referred to as the elites). While this juxtaposition and herding of people into camps might be an effective tool for clickbait and the winning of elections, it's terrible at achieving sovereignty for one simple reason:

It requires trust in a leader to represent the populist masses. Oddly enough, though, this representative leader is almost always from the "class" that they're opposing. Rather than a movement of inner strength and empowerment (a recognition of fundamental, eternal truths), populism is born of a frustration with both perceived and actual weakness and seeks to thrust the burden onto someone deemed capable of "winning" for the people.

Populism is a logical result of people who long for a return to what they know in their gut is "right," but who are so far separated from their sovereign nature that they erroneously believe that other men need to either allow or provide for their liberty. Throughout history, those on the side of control have continually sought to separate man from his innate sovereignty for one very simple reason: it works.

According to a recent Gallup survey, only 30 percent of Americans say they regularly attend religious services of any faith (2021–2023). This marks a 12-percentage point decline from 2000–2003.[11]

Faith in God—or any "higher being"—is declining at an alarming rate, with attacks coming from both ideological (there's no such thing as truth; I am what I say I am) and scientific camps (the more we learn about the human brain, the more we realize we're just algorithms; we're not as special as we think we are). With advances in artificial intelligence (AI) and bioengineering, we can literally play god when we so choose. Even the rise of spirituality (rather than faith) among younger generations is ultimately just a turning inward—to oneself—for answers.

And let's be honest—getting God out of the picture is the all-critical step one. You see, you can't have God-given rights without God. And if our rights aren't unalienable and endowed by our Creator, then they can be debated. Then other men can tell us if and when and under exactly what circumstances those rights can be allowed or suspended. This, in a nutshell, is the meaning of negative liberties—the government can't grant or control our life, liberty, and the pursuit of happiness because they are unarguably and exclusively ours as sovereign individuals. Unlike other nations, who positively grant the "rights" their citizens have, Americans are to be a people who don't allow other men—no matter their stature—to control us. Even the powers ceded to government in the US Constitution are merely to protect these innate rights from infringement by other men. Hence, the moment that government is no longer serving its people by protecting our unalienable rights, it's ripe for disruption.

This is not a battle of right versus left, rich versus poor, or educated versus not. Whether we sit at the bottom of the income quintile or comfortably with the ruling class at the very top, every one of us must decide if we're going to help usher in the next Dark Ages or the next Renaissance. A return to fundamental truth requires stripping every issue down to its core, where we'll almost always find a battle of freedom versus control. Good versus evil. In each instance, we must choose freedom. We must choose good. And we must know why we so choose. Only in doing so will we begin to fill the gaping hole that's become omnipresent in so many of us.

Economic Quintiles

An economic quintile divides a population into five equal groups based on income or wealth, with each quintile representing 20 percent of the population, from lowest to highest. This helps analyze income distribution and economic inequality.

CHAPTER TWO | **REVOLUTION**

It is well enough that people of the nation do not understand our banking and monetary system, for if they did, I believe there would be a revolution before tomorrow morning.

—Henry Ford

MONEY | A BRIEF STROLL THROUGH HISTORY

Money is, ultimately, a story of freedom versus control. As they say, let's start at the very beginning.

Imagine you're a skilled spear-maker in a primitive world. You want a pelt to keep warm during the cold nights, but the only thing you have to offer is a spear. The furrier, however, doesn't want a spear in exchange for his pelts. He wants berries, but you're not a gatherer. And so begins the ancient predicament, the clumsy dance of matching wants that is barter. It didn't take long for our ancestors to discover that this system had limitations—it was time-consuming, inefficient, required physical proximity, and was wholly dependent on the coincidence of wants. Not to mention the even more limiting restrictions of seasonality. What's the berry gatherer to do come winter?

Mental ledgers and IOUs worked for a period of time, but really only in small tribes. Humans tend to be honorable among those they know, but as circles widen loyalty dissipates. You can forget trading with competing tribes this way.

In search of a solution, our ancestors turned to commodities—objects considered universally valuable by common consensus. Various ancient societies, spanning from China to Africa to the Americas, found an answer in seashells. These shells, especially cowrie shells in Africa and wampum in North America, became a primitive form of money. Beautiful, durable, and not so easily found, they seemingly ticked all the right boxes. Yet carrying a pocket full of shells had its challenges, and what good is money if it can't be moved around conveniently, or worse, it can break?

Over time, key characteristics of ideal money emerged—it needed to be acceptable (who wants to receive something they don't know others will want from them?), durable (able to withstand the sands of time and the wear and tear of handling), fungible (all must be uniform and interchangeable, like for like), divisible (easily broken into smaller pieces for varying units of account), recognizable (such that it can be easily accepted without requiring testing or verification), portable (value decreases significantly if you can't take your money with you and have it available when you need it), and scarce (rarity equates value).

Thus, the most salable (i.e., sellable and desirable) good available in a market economy became the soundest money.

If there's any one concept critical to understanding sound money, it's stock-to-flow. Quite simply, it's the ratio of the current stock (i.e., circulating supply) of a commodity versus the flow of new production of said commodity. If you think about it logically, dramatically increasing the supply of anything makes it more common, thus, decreasing its value. Gold has the highest stock-to-flow ratio of any known commodity, with annual production rates hovering around 1.5 percent to 2 percent.[12]

While the concept of stock-to-flow was not defined until much later in history, our innate understanding of it led to the rise of metals as the soundest of the commodity monies—particularly, silver and gold. Note that gold clearly outperforms silver in most every attribute of sound money, with the exception of divisibility. Improvements in technology, namely paper currencies, ultimately made up for this deficiency. This allowed gold, the far sounder form of money with a higher stock-to-flow ratio, to win the long-term metal wars. These same paper currencies also solved other criticisms of gold, such as weight and portability, the need to secure it in vaults, and the need to verify authenticity and purity.

But back to the ancients. . . . The early Egyptians had a penchant for gold, finding that it not only best met the aforementioned characteristics of money and, we now recognize, has a high stock-to-flow ratio, but it was also eminently capable of performing three critical functions of money: It could actually store the value of something, it was a physical medium of exchange, and it was a clear unit of account. Gold became the standard. And the ancient Greeks and Romans, who were great admirers of Egyptian civilization, took the practice to new heights by innovating further and introducing the concept of minting. The Greeks, and later, the Romans, created gold (and other metal) coins and inscribed them with the ruler's image to certify the weight and purity of the metal. No more haggling over the weight of your gold nuggets at the marketplace. More importantly, this simple act allowed their societies to travel through "space and time"—space, in that new peoples could be introduced to Greek and Roman society via their portable coinage, and time, in that the value of their coinage exists yesterday, today, and tomorrow.

While gold was the hardest and most sound of the known commodity monies, it wasn't exclusively used by our ancestors. Salt, grains, livestock, and other metals are all examples of widely used commodity-based systems. And of course, shells. Wampum shells were so prevalent in North America in the early 1600s that arriving colonists to New England's shores developed a fixed exchange rate of shells to their own metal coins.[13] And many African societies recognized cowrie shells as money up until the late nineteenth century. Like so many other commodities, shells were used until technology (the industrial revolution being the final disruption) made this exchange unworkable by flooding the markets with shells, which of course, disrupted the stock-to-flow ratios that had worked for these societies.

It is understandable that industrialized societies always disrupt pre- and lesser-industrialized societies, along with their money, due to their advanced technical abilities to increase the supply of whatever money is currently in use. The period of time it takes for the lesser-advanced society to realize this—that they're being "overtaken"—usually, and unfortunately, becomes a period of great exploitation prior to the collapse of their monetary system.

GOVERNMENT MONEY | THE GREAT CON

Let's take a moment and differentiate between private money—often referred to as market money—and public, or government, money—often referred to as fiat. The term is a Latin word that means "let it be done"; it was used in the sense of an order, a resolution, or a decree. The monetary system underlying fiat is political. Essentially it is government money, a designation of which created a momentous shift in the history of money and, for that matter, of human societies. Prior to the introduction of government, or fiat, money, everything else was previously tied to commodities and was in the hands of the private sector and its free markets. Commodity-based market money has intrinsic value, whereas fiat money has no such intrinsic value since it is based only on the word of the issuing government—for better or worse.

Fiat money also meant the introduction of fiat currency. Currencies are simply standardized mediums of exchange. They can have intrinsic value, such as commodity-based currencies (think of gold coins), they can be legally exchangeable for something with intrinsic value such as representative currencies (think of dollars backed by and redeemable for gold or some other commodity), or they can have only nominal value such as fiat currencies (think of today's dollars backed only by the word of the US government).

First Paper Currency

We can thank the Chinese for the paper currency we use today. No commodities are easy to store in large volumes or transport by individuals. Thus, the concept of a representative currency emerged.

In the seventh century, the Tang dynasty introduced a simple idea: Metal coinage could be deposited in a repository and a paper note issued in exchange. And later, upon returning a note to the repository, the act would reverse, and the metal coinage would be returned. This was particularly convenient for merchants looking to avoid the heavy bulk of copper coinage in large commercial transactions.

The Chinese were the first to attempt a fiat currency—one where a valueless item is widely accepted as a means of payment. The Song dynasty (which ruled from 960 to 1279) introduced what appeared at first to be a representative currency. Paper notes (known as *jiaozi*[14]) were valued at a certain exchange rate for gold, silver, or silk.

However, the government never allowed people to actually convert the paper notes for these commodities, and thus, it wasn't a true representative currency. The plan was for the government to redeem the notes after three years of being in circulation and replace them with new notes for a 3 percent service charge. That plan never materialized. Alas, more and more paper currency was printed without retiring the old notes in exchange, which ultimately flooded the market and devalued the currency. Thus, not too dissimilar to today's government-issued paper, the first attempt at fiat currency got its beginning masked as representative currency and ultimately resulted in inflation and disfavor.

Kublai Khan and his succeeding Yuan dynasty again issued a fiat paper currency—this time without the disguise of being a representative currency. Accounts of this Chinese paper made its way to Europe in the thirteenth century thanks to travelers, such as Marco Polo, who recorded their accounts during the Yuan dynasty. In his book *The Travels of Marco Polo*, Polo included a chapter titled, "How the Great Kaan Causeth the Bark of Trees, Made into Something Like Paper, to Pass for Money All Over his Country." In it, he states,

> All these pieces of paper are, issued with as much solemnity and authority as if they were of pure gold or silver . . . with these pieces of paper, made as I have described, Kublai Khan causes all payments on his own account to be made; and he makes them to pass current

universally over all his kingdoms and provinces and territories, and whithersoever his power and sovereignty extends . . . and indeed everybody takes them readily, for wheresoever a person may go throughout the Great Kaan's dominions he shall find these pieces of paper current, and shall be able to transact all sales and purchases of goods by means of them just as well as if they were coins of pure gold.[15]

Thus, the great con had begun.

It's critical to understand that fiat *money*, such as that of Khan's Yuan dynasty, is different than fiat *currency*. A currency is merely the medium of exchange for its underlying monetary system. And let's be honest, fiat currency is here to stay.

The realities of today's geopolitical landscapes are such that as long as we have nation states, we'll likely have fiat currencies. What's critical is the underlying monetary system.

Fiat money consistently fails due to inflation, which debases the value of the currency. If the debasement is gradual, it often gives people a false sense of productivity rather than the true sense of outright theft by the issuing government. Think about it. It feels good when your salary increases or when you check in on your stock portfolio and see higher numbers. And you feel like you made a smart decision when the internet real estate listing site shows that your home price has increased substantially from just a few years ago. Yet by the same measure, you now have to pay more to acquire those same goods, like houses and equities. So, was it really a win? When food, energy, and our daily necessities cost more, that false sense of productivity is replaced by the reality of the outright theft by the issuing government. Perhaps the people who feel it the most are the younger generations, who are looking to build a life but simply can't do so due to the "false" high costs of the new reality.

This is what we're seeing now, both in the US and globally. And without the market encountering a healthy reset (aka a market crash), which would allow them to enter at a less inflationary price, younger generations will never be able to experience ownership of these assets in the way their parents did. And since no one wants to be at the helm when a reset takes place, we kick the can down the road by printing and issuing more money, making the problem even worse. At least it's someone else's problem, though. Right?

You might have heard people talk about gold and the tale of a fine man's suit. In short, a hundred years ago, an ounce of gold bought a beautiful, well-tailored man's suit. The funny thing is, it still does today. This is because market money is a social consensus, and an ounce of gold is what the market has decided a fine man's suit costs. However, that same suit costs more in fiat money each year because the fiat itself is worth less and less as it is debased. Only sound market money can ensure freedom from meddling and intervention that leads to such debasement.

Inflation and Monetary Debasement

Inflation is the *rate* at which the general level of prices for goods and services rises, reducing the purchasing power of money over time. It occurs when demand outstrips supply or when there is an excessive increase in the money supply.

We measure inflation by tracking the change in prices for a basket of goods and services over time. In the US, the Bureau of Labor Statistics (BLS) measures inflation every month using two main metrics:

- Headline inflation, which includes everything, like food and energy, and
- Core inflation, which excludes those more volatile categories.

Here's a key point—when the rate of inflation lowers, prices are still rising, just at a slower pace. For example, inflation might drop from 8 percent to 3 percent, but that doesn't mean prices are going down. It just means they're rising more slowly. We've seen this recently, with inflation rates cooling from their pandemic highs, but groceries and housing costs are still up from a few years ago.

Inflation can be caused by multiple things. Sometimes it's natural, like when a supply shock—from a disaster, war, or other disruption—limits the availability of goods. Prices rise because supply is down, but demand stays the same.

This kind of inflation is part of the free market responding to changes in supply and demand and is healthy.

But there's another, more unhealthy form of inflation. This happens when governments want to spend more than they have. To cover that gap, they print more money or engage in loose monetary and fiscal policies, flooding the economy with the new money, which causes each unit to become worth less in the open market, thus reducing the overall value of the money. This is known as monetary debasement.

When referring to metal coinage, debasement involves reducing the precious metal content of the coins, often by mixing in less valuable metals or decreasing the coin's weight. This process diminishes the intrinsic value of the coins while maintaining their face value, effectively reducing the worth of the coinage currency in real terms.

DEBASEMENT | IT'S JUST TOO EASY

History has taught us that any monetary system can be debased if it is under centralized control. This debasement is what has brought about the fall of every great civilization since time began. Let's take the Roman Republic. Julius Caesar created the aureus coin, which contained 8 grams of gold and led to a prolonged period of economic stability. This was in addition to the widely circulated Roman denarius silver coin, which contained 3.9 grams of silver. The economic stability was so great that it continued even after the tumultuous transition of the Roman Republic to the Roman Empire and throughout Augustus's reign. It wasn't until Nero came to power that the now infamous habit of Roman "coin clipping" began.

Like any politician, Nero wanted to buy favor with his citizens who had become increasingly reliant on the state and, at the same time, to finance his conquests. His clever solution? Well, it's not much different than what modern economists have advised governments since World War I to do—debase and inflate the money ever-so-slightly by putting more of it into circulation. But unlike our modern governments, Nero was dealing with actual gold and silver, whose pesky stock-to-flow ratios were governed by nature and not man. So he gathered all of the coinage, melted them down, and struck new coins, but with a reduced metal content in each. Occasionally, physical scraping was used to reduce the metal content of older existing coins; these scraps were then combined together to mint new coins on behalf of Nero's government. In doing so, he lowered the aureus from 8 gram to 7.2 grams and the denarius from 3.9 to 3.41.

With the genie out of the bottle, there was no going back. A government having troubles at home or abroad? Debase and inflate a little more. And more. And more. Until it's too late.

Eventually the aureus coin became so severely clipped that a replacement coin was issued, and the solidus gold coin entered circulation with only 4.5 grams of gold. And the silver denarius? Well, it became a farce, with only *traces* of silver covering what had become a bronze core. And that silver would wear off so quickly with use that its acceptance simply ended. The western Roman Empire continued its economic and broader associated cultural deterioration and finally collapsed in AD 476.

That was the *western* empire, but what many people don't realize is what we now call the Byzantine Empire was actually the *eastern* Roman Empire, and it continued for well over a thousand years after the fall of western Rome. How was this possible? Constantine the Great, the first Christian emperor, took the helm and implemented immediate and severe economic reforms. At the same time, he moved the seat of power to Constantinople (modern-day Istanbul, where Europe meets Asia). He maintained the solidus (later known as the bezant) at 4.5 grams of gold without debasement, ultimately turning it into the longest circulating sound currency in history.

Of course, Constantinople eventually came to an end after it, too, began debasing its currency, debasement ultimately leading to its conquest by the Ottomans in 1453. (It's interesting to note that the bezant inspired the Islamic dinar, which, while not the official currency of any nation, is still in circulation in the Islamic world today.)

We've seen this same story play out time and again, the story of societal prosperity followed by cultural and geopolitical tumult, each stemming from an age of sound money to a period of monetary debasement, respectively. But it didn't end with the ancients. We see it in modern history too.

Let's take the period commencing at the end of the Franco-Prussian War in 1871. Historians refer to it as Europe's Belle Epoque (meaning beautiful era) due to its unrivaled prosperity and innovation. This period also saw the peaceful expansion of the British Empire, or Pax Britannica. It's natural for people to want one money to facilitate trade across borders, so during this period, most of Europe came onto a gold standard. The US rejoined a gold standard in 1879, kicking off our own Gilded Age of enlightenment. Paper fiat currencies were the norm by this time, but, as the currencies were representative of a gold monetary system, it was easy to make the conversions. For example, the British pound was equivalent to 7.3 grams of gold, while the French franc was 0.29 grams of gold. Therefore, trade was easy—just do the math. By 1900, roughly fifty countries were on this gold standard, and the sound money financed much of the disruptive technology that shapes our modern way of life.

It all began to erode with the centralization of control over gold via modern central banks, such as the Federal Reserve in the US and its counterparts around the world like the Bank of England in the UK. And the adherence to a gold standard came to an end in 1914 with the outbreak of WWI. (Only Sweden and Switzerland, which remained neutral during the war, remained on the gold standard for several more years.)

There was now a war that needed to be financed and—well, we know how this story goes. Centralization of control over large amounts of the gold in circulation meant that governments could issue more paper currency than was actually backed by their gold. And given the alternative of taxation or confiscation of their citizens' money—which would have made going to war much more unpopular to the citizenry—those in charge elected to instead debase and inflate their currencies to finance their part in the Great War. Within mere weeks of the outbreak of fighting, all participating nations had abandoned the gold standard in favor of a fiat money system, which they could completely control. You see, with the suspension of redeemability to gold (meaning, paper money could not be exchanged, or "redeemed," for gold), those in control were no longer limited to the actual money in their countries—whether in their central banks or via their citizens' wealth. They could print whatever was needed to finance whatever was desired.

Global war simply isn't possible without a fiat money system. We could never afford it.

Fast forward to the end of World War II—the point at which the United States essentially transitioned from a republic to an empire. To the victor go the spoils. And America, having decisively ended the bloody war, wanted more than her fair share.

Summoning nearly two dozen allied nations to Bretton Woods, New Hampshire, US leaders insisted upon the creation of a new global monetary system whereby dollars would be used as the world's reserve currency (i.e., used by other nations' central banks). Their currencies could be convertible to dollars at fixed rates, and those dollars could further be converted to gold at a fixed rate. This system saw the

US Federal Reserve take in gold from other central banks in exchange for dollars at a rate of $35 per ounce, further solidifying American dominance. (At the time of this writing, that same ounce of gold is trading at around $2,400 USD. That's one very expensive suit!) Note that while the US and the other nations involved in Bretton Woods understood that gold needed to play a part, this was really an act of central planning. It was the antithesis of the free-market, gold-commodity money, which had produced ages of mass prosperity and innovation through history. Because this central planning wasn't a true gold standard, American citizens couldn't redeem their dollars for gold. In fact, citizens were prevented from even owning gold until 1974.[16]

Instead, this was a game between central banks. And that game needed rules and referees. Thus, Bretton Woods also established the World Bank and the International Monetary Fund (IMF), the latter tasked with coordinating between central banks to achieve stable exchange rates and financial flows. Such coordination was necessary since, unlike the gold-backed trade of the pre-WWI era wherein one could simply do the math, it was assumed that post-WWII governments had a right to continually engineer their domestic economies.

The US dollar inevitably declined under this post-war era of financial engineering, and other nations sought to repatriate their gold. In the end, the US defaulted on its gold redemption commitment. On August 15, 1971, President Richard Nixon announced the end of the central bank gold standard.

The following graph describes the situation after even that tenuous link to sound money was broken. There's a reason those seeking to dethrone the dollar as the reserve are heavily purchasing gold via their own central banks and slowly re-backing their currencies.

A DOLLAR'S WORTH: PURCHASING POWER OF THE US DOLLAR

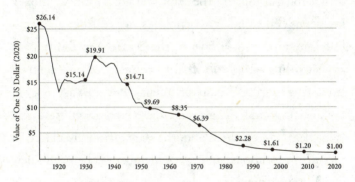

Source: *Visual Capitalist, https://www.visualcapitalist.com/purchasing-power-of-the-u-s-dollar-over-time.*

BITCOIN | NEW PARADIGM, OLD CONCEPT

Technology disrupts and marches ever onward. We've seen it in the ancient world, where commodities displaced early mental ledgers as a superior form of money, and we've seen it throughout the ages, where industrialized societies displaced pre- and lesser-industrialized societies and their forms of money. Today, as the digital disrupts the analog, it's only natural that a digital form of money would emerge.

Built on the proverbial shoulders of giants, bitcoin is the first truly digital solution to money. Unlike the digital cash we commonly interact with, which is merely showing a digital abstraction or copy, bitcoin is digitally native.

Interestingly, bitcoin is simultaneously disruptive and reminiscent of the earliest mental ledger money primitives.

The best example of these primitive mental ledgers comes from the island of Yap (part of the Federated States of Micronesia today). The Yapese used a form of money known as Rai stones, circular disks carved from a crystalline limestone with a hole in the center. Yap didn't have any such limestone, so it had to be quarried and shipped from neighboring Guam or Palau—not an easy feat in the ancient world. As a result, these stones were rare and valuable. Once on the island, the Rai stones were placed in prominent locations, and every member of the tribe knew which stone belonged to whom. The owner of a stone could use it as payment by announcing an ownership change. The Yapese would all take mental note of this new ownership— keeping and constantly updating a mental ledger. This primitive form of money worked for centuries until—as you can now guess—the arrival of a more industrialized people, who were able to easily import Rai stones and who ended up flooding the market and devaluing them.[17]

As a digital asset, bitcoin is similar to the Yapese's mental ledger. The coins themselves never really move. It's the ownership that transfers.

It's not important to understand the intricacies of *how* bitcoin works any more than it is to understand the chemical properties of gold or how it is mined. Yet there are three concepts that are critical to understanding *why* bitcoin so perfectly checks all the boxes of sound and sovereign money in a digital age: self-custody, trust, and difficulty adjustment.

Sovereign individuals have always sought money that needs no permissions. Gold and physical cash are both bearer assets—meaning that the person holding the asset has all the benefits of ownership. This fundamental feature of self-custody has been attacked by governments throughout history, as it removes the effectiveness of third-party controls. Bitcoin is also a bearer asset. But keep in mind that it's a digitally native asset, so it will only ever exist as an entry on the Bitcoin network's ledger. What you possess are the rights to control the entries (and thus sell or transfer control of the coins) pertaining to the amount of bitcoin that you own. We call these rights *keys*, but they're nothing more than numbers represented as a series of twelve to twenty-four words.

Bitcoin Keys

Bitcoin keys consist of a private key and a public key.

The private key is a secret number that allows you to transfer your bitcoin, while the public key is derived from the private key and is used to receive bitcoin. For example, if your private key is like a password that grants access to your funds, your public key is like an email address you share to receive payments.

Typically, the private key is represented as a series of twelve to twenty-four words, known as a seed phrase or mnemonic phrase, which encodes the private key in a more human-readable form. While the underlying private key itself is a large, random number, the seed phrase is used to generate and secure that key in a way that is easier to back up and remember.

Are you confused by bitcoin terminology? You're not alone. Bitcoin was developed by coders and without the influence of marketing teams. As such, the words the industry uses are often as clear as mud. For example, the various software that generate the seed phrases used to protect keys are known as *wallets*, the idea being that people would intuitively associate a wallet with where their money was. But since bitcoin is digitally native, you never physically possess it (only the rights to control it), and it never moves from its native blockchain. When someone refers to transferring bitcoin, those coins aren't moving from one wallet to another. Your wallet never "has" your bitcoin. Only the right to control the movement of those coins is being transferred and is being recorded on the bitcoin blockchain ledger.

Use of the term *wallet* was a terrible idea and has resulted in a common misunderstanding about how bitcoin (and all digitally native assets) work. After all, who thinks of their wallet as storing their keys?

Think back to how paper currencies helped to solve some of gold's deficiencies in divisibility, weight, and portability. Bitcoin has no such deficiencies. While there will only ever be 21 million bitcoin, each bitcoin is divided into 100,000,000 *satoshis* (equaling 2.1 quadrillion *satoshis*). These are named after bitcoin's pseudonymous founder "Satoshi Nakamoto" and are commonly known as *sats*. The keys to the entries regarding these whole bitcoins or sats are what a person can own and, thus, what one can self-custody. Keys weigh nothing, and portability is not an issue. They can even be self-custodied across national borders with nothing to declare. After all, it's just words in your head.

Transacting in physical cash or physical gold doesn't require anyone's permission. The transaction settles instantly with no risk of charge-back. What it does require is physical proximity of the parties to the transaction. Hence the development of third-party intermediaries and solutions such as banks and their associated cards, wires, ACH transfers, and checks, and neobanks like CashApp, Venmo, and PayPal. While these intermediated payments are far more convenient and facilitate our modern way of life, they have removed a fundamental characteristic of sovereign money and inserted a third party that now must be trusted. These trusted third parties can place limits on liquidity, surveil and report on user activity, and as we'll see in later chapters, ultimately determine if, when, where, and how you can spend your own money. Far from ideal.

Bitcoin solved this issue of trust with radical transparency, allowing anyone and everyone to verify its ledger, tracing back to the first sale of bitcoins in October 2009. This provides proof and verification, as every transaction must be recorded by every computer hosting a full copy of the Bitcoin blockchain, ensuring they all share one single and universally accepted ledger.

The concept is simple: As a self-custodied bearer asset, bitcoin requires no intermediaries to settle its transactions. And the process of recording those transactions is intentionally difficult and energy intensive, requiring massive computing power to solve a mathematical problem before the information can be recorded. Once the problem is solved by one computer, a majority of the other computers must vote to accept it as true, and then all copies of the ledger are updated with the information (just as all Yapese would update their mental ledger with a Rai stone's new ownership after an announcement).

This happens roughly every ten minutes, with each recorded bit of data known as a block and stored in a chained linear fashion after the previous one. Hence, *blockchain*. And as you can imagine, it becomes harder and harder to reverse any accepted block when new blocks of information are added since a majority of the computers hosting the ledger would need to agree with this new version of events.

In addition, dishonesty isn't rewarded in such a system. On a smaller scale, if an individual or a small group of bad actors attempted to tamper with a transaction or create a false version of the ledger, their efforts would be futile. The corrupted copy of the ledger would simply be thrown out and ignored by the majority of honest computers because it failed the rigorous validation checks. On a larger scale, suppose a scenario occurred where a majority of the network (51 percent or more) conspired to alter the blockchain for malicious purposes. Even if this majority succeeded in its treachery, it would have failed in its ultimate endeavor to gain value or make a profit, as the false transactions and associated coins would have no value now that the network's security had been breached. Bitcoin's value is derived from the integrity of the Bitcoin network.

Finally, it's in understanding not just the laws of economics but of human nature, too, that the real stroke of genius in bitcoin's code lies. History has taught us that when something is valuable, men will do anything possible to produce more of it for gain. Gold has preserved its high stock-to-flow ratio despite human nature thanks to the natural laws that constrain it. As a digital asset, bitcoin would need a way to hardcode these laws. You see, it's not enough that there would only ever be twenty-one million bitcoin. Satoshi Nakamoto needed a way to prevent them from being issued too quickly, thus flooding the market and devaluing the money. Enter the difficulty adjustment.

Recall that new blocks of transactions are recorded roughly every ten minutes. This process is what triggers the release of new bitcoins into the network as a reward for the computer that solved the mathematical problem first. The number of coins released is also hardcoded, beginning with fifty coins in the first four years and continually halved every four years after that. The result is that the first twenty million bitcoin will have been released by 2025, but the last one million will take roughly another one hundred years.

With the number of coins hardcoded, the aspect that could seemingly be tampered with is the block time. Logically, the dedication of more processing power to figuring out the mathematical equations faster should mean that the ten-minute increments could be sped up, thereby releasing the coins faster and faster. And there would be an ever-increasing incentive for doing so as more people choose to hold bitcoin, making it more and more valuable. But instead, as the processing power rises, bitcoin raises the difficulty of the problems needing to be solved—ensuring that it always takes roughly ten minutes to do so. The more you try to scam the network, the more secure it becomes.

Bitcoin is money and a compelling sovereign asset. In our digital age, how salable will the asset become? How sound will this money be? Only time will tell.

Let's close here with words of Nobel laureate economist Friedrich Hayek:

> I don't believe that we shall ever have a good money again before we take the thing out of the hands of government. Since we can't take them violently out of the hands of government, all we can do is by some sly roundabout way introduce something they can't stop.[18]

And of Ralph Merkle, inventor of the Merkle tree data structure:

Bitcoin is the first example of a new form of life. It lives and breathes on the internet. It lives because it can pay people to keep it alive. It lives because it performs a useful service that people will pay it to perform. It lives because anyone, anywhere, can run a copy of its code. It lives because all the running copies are constantly talking to each other. It lives because if any one copy is corrupted it is discarded, quickly and without any fuss or muss. It lives because it is radically transparent: anyone can see its code and see exactly what it does. It can't be changed. It can't be argued with. It can't be tampered with. It can't be corrupted. It can't be stopped. It can't even be interrupted. If nuclear war destroyed half of our planet, it would continue to live, uncorrupted. It would continue to offer its services. It would continue to pay people to keep it alive. The only way to shut it down is to kill every server that hosts it. Which is hard, because a lot of servers host it, in a lot of countries, and a lot of people want to use it. Realistically, the only way to kill it is to make the service it offers so useless and obsolete that no one wants to use it. So obsolete that no one wants to pay for it. No one wants to host it. Then it will have no money to pay anyone. Then it will starve to death. But as long as there are people who want to use it, it's very hard to kill, or corrupt, or stop, or interrupt.[19]

CHAPTER THREE | **CIVICS**

Only a virtuous people are capable of freedom.
—Benjamin Franklin

AMERICA | DO WE REALLY KNOW HER?

America's greatness can be largely attributed to its founding principles and ensuing documents. These are grounded in fundamental truth and express an exquisite understanding of human nature.

Unfortunately, over time, there have been deviations from these foundational principles. Sometimes, the deviations are so gradual that they are almost imperceptible, but other times, the changes are drastic, where human nature has succumbed to its weaknesses. The ever-increasing power of the federal government, often at the expense of states' rights and individual freedoms, is now a point of vehement contention. The original vision of a limited government, primarily focused on protecting rights and freedoms, has been overshadowed by political and bureaucratic expansions, which are ever encroaching on these liberties under the guise of "protecting" the people. The divisive political climate of the late 2010s and early 2020s has led to a departure from the ideals of natural law and the governance outlined in the Constitution. And the increasing polarization and partisanship challenges the collaborative civic spirit envisioned by our founding fathers. This straying from core values and principles raises concerns about the future direction of America—both as a nation and an idea.

Even after it was enshrined in America's Constitution as such, Thomas Jefferson continued to advocate for a federal government that was "reduced to a very simple organization, and a very inexpensive one; a few plain duties to be performed by a few servants."[20]

Does this sound like the America you know?

Many today believe America is defined by corruption, control, greed, and lies—the antithesis of all that is good in the world. Her own people are seeking to tear her down because of it. But is it really America they detest?

For some, yes. Ideology runs deep, and our society has indoctrinated entire generations by using the techniques we'll soon be discussing. But for others, what they understand as America is really just a perversion. In short, the living, breathing embodiment of our Founders' worst nightmares.

Words matter. It's high time we all learn what the hell we're talking about.

NATURAL LAW | TRUE, TIMELESS, AND UNIVERSAL

The Roman man Marcus Tullius Cicero (106–43 BC) was the first to envision a model society based on natural law and is easily the American Founders' favorite expositor on the subject. He studied law in Rome, philosophy in Athens, and ultimately rose to the high office of Roman Consul. His writings have endured throughout the ages, in particular his seminal works, *De Re Publica* (On the Republic) and *De Legibus* (On the Laws). There is good reason why his stance on what natural law is has lasted for centuries:

> True law is right reason in agreement with nature; it is of universal application, unchanging and everlasting; it summons to duty by its commands, and averts from wrongdoing by its prohibitions . . . It is a sin to try to alter this law, nor is it allowable to repeal any part of it, and it is impossible to abolish it entirely. We cannot be freed from its obligations by senate or people, and we need not look outside ourselves for an expounder or interpreter of it. And there will not be different laws at Rome and at Athens, or different laws now and in the future, but one eternal and unchangeable law will be valid for all nations and all times, and there will be one master and ruler, that is God, over us all, for he is the author of this law, its promulgator, and its enforcing judge. Whoever is disobedient is fleeing from himself and denying his human nature, and by reason of this very fact he will suffer the worst punishment.[21]

Cicero came to believe that there must be a Creator behind the universe and that this divine being had set an order to things—an immutable code woven into the very fabric of existence known as natural law. This universal principle transcends the ephemeral edicts of man-made legislation and remains accessible to all who seek to discern its truths. Under natural law, the commonsense approach is often the correct one, since conclusions are often based on reason and a "fundamental presupposition of Natural Law is that man's reasoning power is a special dispensation of the Creator and is closely akin to the rational or reasoning power of the Creator himself."[22]

Cicero wasn't alone in his appreciation of natural law. English philosopher John Locke, a prominent Enlightenment figure, put it this way:

The state of Nature has a law of Nature to govern it, which . . . teaches all mankind who will but consult it, that being all equal and independent, no one ought to harm another in his life, health, liberty, or possessions; for men being all the workmanship of one omnipotent and infinitely wise maker; all the servants of one sovereign master, sent into the world by His order and about His business; they are His property . . . And, being furnished with like faculties, sharing all in one community of Nature, there cannot be supposed any such subordination among us that may authorize us to destroy one another.[23]

Respected contemporaries of our Founders in the 1700s, such as the English jurist, justice, politician, and scholar William Blackstone, believed it was the only reliable basis for a system of justice. And while they may have disagreed on much, the writings of all the early American revolutionaries were full of references to natural law and its critical importance as the basis for a just and stable society.

From natural law, we get the concepts of unalienable rights and duties, *habeas corpus*, no taxation without representation, the right to contract, limited government, separation of powers, checks and balances, and many others. In short, America is grounded in natural law.

Through his dialogues and treatises, Cicero elucidates the interplay between natural law and human conduct. He exhorts individuals to heed the dictates of conscience and aspire to loftier ideals. In his vision, the pursuit of justice, virtue, and the common good is intertwined with an unwavering fidelity to this transcendent moral order.

The American Founders embraced this thinking wholeheartedly and set about building a moral and virtuous society—a requisite in their minds to the system of government they hoped to pursue. It may seem laughable today but leading up to 1776, the biggest question for most of the colonists was one of worthiness. Were they as a people sufficiently moral and virtuous to govern themselves? Were they good enough? After all, it was universally accepted that a corrupt and selfish people were incapable of self-government.

Some have likened the early American concept of "public virtue" to the Golden Rule. Others have termed it a willingness of individuals to sacrifice their own desires for the good of the community—patriotism over personal wants. So many people became concerned over their lack of public virtue that it brought about a massive virtuous reform movement throughout all thirteen colonies. Fascinatingly, this reform movement might have even hastened the revolution.

Earlier skeptics like John Jay and Robert Morris (Morris being one of only two men to sign all three of America's founding documents) began to believe that self-government might be possible as people everywhere began to exhibit virtuous potential and improve their social consciousness. Meanwhile, the colonists became nervous that if they didn't separate from the corrupt English soon, they might lose their newfound leanings.

Perhaps in this context, and with a proper understanding of natural law, the many warnings about the inevitable loss of liberty should we fail to be a deserving and virtuous people make a little more sense.

Samuel Adams, the Father of the American Revolution, once wrote to a friend, "I thank God that I have lived to see my country independent and free. She may long enjoy her independence and freedom if she will. It depends on her virtue."[24]

His cousin John Adams agreed, and were he here today, would have no trouble understanding our current predicament. He said, "Our Constitution was made only for a moral and religious people. It is wholly inadequate to the government of any other."[25]

You see, virtue cannot be mandated or forced. It must come from free will. Simply passing laws requiring good behavior, punishing corruption, and mandating non-discriminatory practices doesn't cut it. It simply invites more laws and regulations followed by the requisite power-hungry bureaucrats necessary to enforce them. Fast forward a few generations, and what you're left with isn't freedom at all. It's a tangled web of "protections"—protecting you from each other instead of protecting your rights. Sound familiar?

Virtue is not hereditary. If we want to be free, we need to be *capable* of being free. This is the cornerstone of American self-government—something we'd all do well to remember.

SEPARATION OF CHURCH AND STATE |
NOT RELIGION AND STATE

For days in late March 2024, social media was abuzz with heated talk of "Christian Nationalism." One side was incorrectly defining and bashing it. The other was also incorrectly defining it but defending it. Glaringly absent was the chorus of well-educated citizens pointing out that what was being discussed wasn't Christian Nationalism at all.

While building for some time, the debate came to a head when Alexander Ward and Heidi Przybyla published an article in Politico[26] about the dangers of President Trump's allies preparing to infuse Christian Nationalist ideas into his second administration. The article intimated that anyone who read and understood our Declaration of Independence— that our rights come from God and not from a government of men—was an avowed Christian Nationalist.

Heidi Przybyla later went on MSNBC to double down—this time leaving no room for doubt: "The thing that unites them as Christian Nationalists . . . is that they believe that our rights as Americans, as all human beings, don't come from any earthly authority. They don't come from Congress. They don't come from the Supreme Court. They come from God."[27] She continued on, denigrating "that so-called natural law"[28] as the other commentators looked on and nodded gravely that this travesty could be taking place.

This, my friends, is a simple—albeit glaring—failure of American civics.

First, let's get one thing straight. There is such a thing as Christian Nationalism and it's all-caps *BAD*. Christian Nationalism is where the church plays a defining role in the government. In its purest form, it's an actual coupling of church and government. Of church and state.

Many conservatives have suggested that since modern-day America has drifted so far from its moral and religious roots, you need to force the Christian Nationalism agenda first, and only when it is achieved can you back off. This thinking is dangerous. And equally as wrong as where we are today.

America is not a theocracy. Our government and its laws are of men—which is precisely why they are incapable of prescribing our rights, only protecting them.

Judeo-Christian Principles

Judeo-Christian principles refer to the ethical and moral guidelines that originate from the teachings and values shared by both Judaism and Christianity. They emphasize concepts such as the sanctity of human life, moral responsibility, rule of law, the importance of family, and personal freedom and responsibility—all of which America's Founders incorporated into the nation's structure.

A shared religious belief in a common God was never the issue. It was about the principles that provided a foundational framework for organizing society.

For example, upon wise counsel from his father-in-law, Jethro, the law of Moses established a structured, tiered system of governance. It began with the family as the core unit of society, emphasizing the importance of familial bonds, education, and moral responsibility. From there, leadership was organized into small groups, with local leaders overseeing families and communities.

According to Exodus 18:21–25, the ancient Israelites were organized into groups of tens, fifties, hundreds, and thousands:

- Groups of 10: each group of 10 families had a designated leader
- Groups of 50: five groups of 10 families were overseen by another leader
- Groups of 100: two groups of 50 families were managed by a higher-level leader
- Groups of 1,000: ten groups of 100 families fell under the jurisdiction of a senior leader

This structure ensured efficient governance, with responsibilities divided among many leaders and a clear system for escalating only those issues that couldn't be resolved at a lower level. Similarly, under the US Constitution, an emphasis is always placed on the smallest possible unit of governance and dispute resolution—from self to family to community—long before the federal, or even state, government gets involved.

But because most people don't know what Christian Nationalism actually is, it's yet another term that can now be manipulated. Redefined. Even defended by those who would be embarrassed to be associated with its true meaning. (More on this redefining of critical terms later.)

Understanding that your rights come from God and not from men is basic American civics. It's spelled out clearly in our Declaration of Independence. This is why former presidential candidate Vivek Ramaswamy, a Hindu, not only understands this historical, philosophical, and legal truism, but can also speak so eloquently on it. Because he shares the belief, even though he's not a Christian.

So let's understand how we can have God-given rights and still maintain the all-critical separation of church and state.

For starters, it's exactly that—a separation of *church* and state. Religion and state, on the other hand, are very much intertwined. We can understand this by first defining *religion* in the context of civics.

One historian noted that religion can be thought of in this context as a "fundamental system of beliefs concerning man's origin and relationship to the cosmic universe as well as his relationship to his fellowmen." Note that this is different than morality, which can be thought of as a "standard of behavior distinguishing right and wrong."[29]

The thinking was (and is) simple: Religion—a step up from basic morality—makes us better citizens. It instills in us the aforementioned virtue required for freedom to prosper, and it secures our standing *above* any government. In a system of laws founded on negative liberties, we must understand that the system itself recognizes our rights as coming from our Creator.

This is what legal immigrants still denote on their citizenship tests today. Recognizing the role of religion in civics is an acknowledgment that if you believe that statement to be true, not just understand that the system is predicated upon it, you will more jealously guard your unalienable rights as your own—thus, making you a better citizen.

In 1787, the same Congress that ratified the US Constitution that year also set forth the Northwest Ordinance, a system for governing the Northwest Territory, which included areas that would later become the states of Ohio, Indiana, Illinois, Michigan, Wisconsin, and part of Minnesota. It was significant because it provided a blueprint for how new territories could become states, emphasizing principles of representative government and civil liberties. In it, Congress accentuated the need for education, and for religion and morality to be taught alongside knowledge. Article 3 states, "Religion, morality, and knowledge being necessary to good government and the happiness of mankind, schools and the means of education shall forever be encouraged."[30]

The Founders sought religion to be a unifying cultural adhesive, not something to tear us apart. Hence, the consistent affirmation that the government never adopt or endorse a single religion or sect. This leads to the question, then, of *how* religion should be taught to the youth. The religious tenets taught were those deemed fundamental and universally accepted by all faiths—often referred to by the Founders as "the religion of America."[31]

Benjamin Franklin, in a letter to the president of Yale University, laid out these five tenets that were taught in our early schools most clearly: "Here is my creed: I believe in one God, the Creator of the universe. That he governs it by his providence. That he ought to be worshipped. That the most acceptable service we render to him is in doing good to his other children. That the soul of man is immortal, and will be treated with justice in another life respecting its conduct in this. These I take to be the fundamental points in all sound religion."[32]

President George Washington warned us not to lose this ethos in his "Farewell Address," stating, "Of all the dispositions and habits which lead to political prosperity, religion and morality are indispensable supports."[33]

The French jurist Alexis de Tocqueville authored *Democracy in America*, universally heralded as one of the greatest societal and constitutional studies of its time, after a visit to the US in 1831. Throughout his book, he returns time and again to the nature of the American people. Her secret sauce.

> On my arrival in the United States the religious aspect of the country was the first thing that struck my attention; and the longer I stayed there, the more I perceived the great political consequences resulting from this new state of things . . .
>
> Religion in America takes no direct part in the government of society, but it must be regarded as the first of their political institutions . . . I do not know whether all Americans have a sincere faith in their religion—for who can search the human heart?—but I am certain that they hold it to be indispensable to the maintenance of republican institutions. This opinion is not peculiar to a class of citizens or to a party, but it belongs to the whole nation and to every rank of society.[34]

Has America lost her secret sauce?

None of this can be mandated. And all of it is required for our American system of liberty to work.

GOVERNANCE | A CENTRIST APPROACH

Guided by natural law and its ensuing principles, the American Founders set about to discover the ideal form of government. One that was capable of enduring throughout the ages and predicated on an understanding of human nature.

They began their studies with the simple insight that when looking at governments, what really needed to be measured was power. Essentially, control. Thus, they examined all possible forms of government within the context of a spectrum of control, a measurement we still use today. On the extreme left, they placed tyranny; this was 100 percent control by the government. On the extreme right, they placed anarchy; this was 0 percent control by the government. Ultimately, they settled on the direct center of this control spectrum as the ideal. Additionally, they drew from the Anglo-Saxons (common law tradition, local governance, and checks and balances) and Ancient Israelites (republican principles, covenant tradition, and moral law). Goldilocks would have been proud.

American governance is based on all power residing in the people. In short, the people are sovereign, and society is structured for *their* benefit.

English political theorist and politician Algernon Sidney was one of the early and outspoken critics of the concept of the divine right of kings to rule over their lands. Sidney dared to state that sovereignty is actually vested in the people, and therefore, no one can rule them without their consent. This didn't go over well with British royalty, and in 1683 King Charles II beheaded Sidney for his heresy.

Sidney's contemporary John Locke took his cue to exit and fled to Holland. He stayed there in safety until after England's bloodless Glorious Revolution, which he helped plot from afar and which saw the principles of British constitutional monarchy and parliamentary supremacy enshrined. Upon his return to England in 1690, Locke published his essays on civil government, highlighting that power rests on the consent of the people.

Well versed in Locke's writings and again drawing from the Anglo-Saxons and ancient Israelites, America's Founders subscribed to the concept that sovereign authority rests with the people and that the government has power only when, and to the extent, delegated by the people. Thus, the people can elect or remove a ruler within their sole discretion.

It's important to note that while our system of governance vests all power in the people, it's not a democracy. As students of history, America's Founders were well aware of how quickly and easily democracies could turn to tyranny, as power can be gained by exploiting social and economic grievances. They knew well the cautionary tales of Greek city-states such as Athens and Corinth, which may be known as the birthplaces of democracy, but which ended in tyranny.

As James Madison put it: "Democracies have ever been spectacles of turbulence and contention; have ever been found incompatible with personal security or the rights of property; and have in general been as short in their lives as they have been violent in their deaths."[35]

Hence, America's Founders wisely opted for a republican form of government via elected representatives. This decision, more than any other, is probably why our republic still stands today.

It's easy to forget that America didn't get it right on the first try. Her first constitution was a failure. We talk a lot about the power struggles between the people and the federal government, but it was assumed and agreed by all that sovereignty must rest in the people. Of equal or greater concern at the time was the power struggle between the states and the federal government, to whom the people would be delegating their powers.

In the summer of 1776, when it became apparent that separation was the only viable outcome, the Continental Congress appointed a committee to write a constitution even before declaring independence. John Dickinson drafted the Articles of Confederation based off an earlier proposal by Benjamin Franklin in 1775. Dickinson's Articles were not well received by the states, who continued to modify the draft until they were certain the federal government would have no powers except those and only those expressly authorized by the states. And as you can guess, that wasn't much.

This fear of a strong central government resulted in the Articles of Confederation, which, when finally adopted in 1781, sat too close to the anarchy side of the Founders' power scale. General George Washington attributed the death and disease of thousands of his soldiers to the impotence of the central government under the Articles of Confederation.

Luckily, these revolutionaries were men of unwavering principles. They recognized their error and fixed the problem. The ensuing Constitutional Convention in 1787 included non-public debates and implementation of what they called the Committee of the Whole—consisting of all members of the convention, but without any of the formality. This allowed all to speak freely. Only upon reaching consensus would the same group reconstitute as the Convention and formally vote on what had already been decided in Committee.

The Constitutional Convention took four months. Issues weren't forced with less-than-ideal compromises. It took over sixty ballots simply to resolve the presidential election process. The delegates took the time to repeatedly talk through issues until a true meeting of the minds by a vast majority was reached.

On September 17, 1787, George Washington attached a letter to the signed draft of the Constitution and sent it to Congress for ratification, which it did without any changes. It was then sent to the states, which were invited to submit suggestions rather than reject the new Constitution. Wanting to leave no room for doubt as to the limited delegated powers of the new government, they submitted 189, which were thankfully reduced to 12 by James Madison, and 10 of which were approved and ratified by the states as America's Bill of Rights.

Constitutional ratification finally concluded in 1790, when Rhode Island became the final state to do so.

The months and years leading up to America's founding were full of bitter in-fighting among her leaders. The vitriol could rival what we see today. Yet unlike today, the fights were about the practical aspects of implementation and rarely about the underlying principle(s). How is that possible? Some have proffered that it had to do with how well-read they were. America's Founders were familiar with European, English, Anglo-Saxon, Greek, and Roman history. They could quote Polybius, Cicero, Thomas Hooker, Blackstone, John Locke, Montesquieu, and Adam Smith, just to name a few. They could also quote the Bible, in particular, the Old Testament.

But I personally think it has less to do with what they *read* (after all, they were versed in opposing philosophies as well) and more to do with how they *thought*. These men knew how to reason from first principles. America's Founders were products of the Enlightenment, an era where the light of reason pierced through the clouds of superstition and dogma. An era where it was a badge of honor, not just to own a copy of the Bible, but to own the works of John Locke, Isaac Newton, Francis Bacon, and Adam Smith—books not meant to sit decoratively on the table, but to be broken down and studied, something that would encourage a battle with their underlying ideas. These torchbearers were seen as illuminating the path to knowledge, freedom, and progress.

The Enlightenment culture was a product of deep philosophical roots, and America was *the* Enlightenment country, epitomizing the best Modern thought of the day. The air was ripe with ideas about individual rights, scientific inquiry, and secular governance, and this garden of intellectual blossoming is where the seeds of American governance were sown.

What would these champions of liberty think if they saw us today?

Cicero wrote in his work *De Legibus* that the closer the collapse of the empire, the crazier its laws are. America is dangerously close to needing some more thoughtful and well-read principled revolutionaries.

CHAPTER FOUR | **KNOWLEDGE**

*If a nation expects to be ignorant and free, in
a state of civilization, it expects what never
was and never will be.*

—Thomas Jefferson

AMERICA | A NATION AND AN IDEA

The US may be acting like a late-stage empire, but her fate
is not predetermined. Whether or not she survives is very
much up to those of us alive today. America will, inevitably, be humbled in the coming months and years. The
question is whether, after this humbling, she will once
again rise to be great. In this age of misguided collectivism,
can America as a nation find its way to becoming a beacon
for individual liberty?

Of course, America is far more than a nation. She is
a set of ideals ("We hold these truths"). Thus, the critical
question is whether We the People can free America, as an
idea, to not only continue, but to thrive as well. After all,

what good is propping up the body if the light has gone out from within?

The answer lies not with the politicians, but with each of us as citizens. One thing is certain—we can't simply vote our way out of this mess. Only an educated and sovereign populace who is willing to continually assert that sovereignty can rekindle the fire within America's belly and awaken our great nation.

So let's take a moment and rewind the clock. Let's look at the state of American education.

EDUCATION | QUICKLY BECOMING A MISNOMER

America has historically worn her culture of competence as a badge of honor. Every answer might not have been known, but we knew how to problem solve. American ingenuity was undeniable. As a people, we were well read, we were creative, we were curious, and we were proud of these traits.

The promise of the information age was to pour fuel on the fire of these traits. Yet the reality has been anything but. Instead, we find ourselves in a culture where self-help books and informational podcasts abound, teaching us how to extricate ourselves from our electronic devices and the corresponding dopamine hits so we can focus for more than a few minutes. Rather than the norm, focused work is now taught as a contemporary art.

Most people today assume that the eighth-grade education of our great-grandparents must have been pitiful. I mean, think of how much has been discovered and invented since they were young. Yet take a look at the questions below; they made up some of the eighth-grade final exam questions asked in 1895 in Salina, Kansas[36] (not exactly a thriving metropolis). Could you pass this exam?

GRAMMAR (Time, 1 hour)

1. Give nine rules for the use of capital letters.
2. Name the parts of speech and define those that have no modifications.
3. Define verse, stanza, and paragraph.
4. What are the principal parts of a verb? Give principal parts of *lie*, *play*, and *run*.
5. Define case; illustrate each case.
6. What is punctuation? Give rules for principal marks of punctuation.
7. Write a composition of about 150 words and show therein that you understand the practical use of the rules of grammar.

ARITHMETIC (Time, 1 hour 15 minutes)

1. Name and define the Fundamental Rules of Arithmetic.
2. A wagon box is 2 ft. deep, 10 ft. long, and 3 ft. wide. How many bushels of wheat will it hold?
3. If a load of wheat weighs 3,942 lbs. What is it worth at 50cts/bushel, deducting 1,050 lbs. for tare?

4. District No. 33 has a valuation of $35,000. What is the necessary levy to carry on a school seven months at $50 per month, and have $104 for incidentals?

5. Find the cost of 6,720 lbs. coal at $6.00 per ton.

6. Find the interest of $512.60 for 8 months and 18 days at 7 percent per annum.

7. What is the cost of 40 boards 12 inches wide and 16 ft. long at $20 per metre?

8. Find the bank discount on $300 for 90 days (no grace) at 10 percent.

9. What is the cost of a square farm at $15 per acre, the distance of which is 640 rods?

10. Write a Bank Check, a Promissory Note, and a Receipt.

US HISTORY (Time, 45 minutes)

1. Give the epochs into which US History is divided

2. Give an account of the discovery of America by Columbus.

3. Relate the causes and results of the Revolutionary War.

4. Show the territorial growth of the United States . . .

5. Tell what you can of the history of Kansas

6. Describe three of the most prominent battles of the Rebellion.

7. Who were the following: Morse, Whitney, Fulton, Bell, Lincoln, Penn, and Howe?

8. Name events connected with the following dates: 1607, 1620, 1800, 1849, 1865.

ORTHOGRAPHY (Time, 1 hour)

1. What is meant by the following: alphabet, phonetic, orthography, etymology, syllabication?
2. What are elementary sounds? How classified?
3. What are the following, and give examples of each: trigraph, subvocals, diphthong, cognate letters, linguals?
4. Give four substitutes for caret *u*.
5. Give two rules for spelling words with final *e*. Name two exceptions under each rule.
6. Give two uses of silent letters in spelling. Illustrate each.
7. Define the following prefixes and use in connection with a word: bi, dis, pre, semi, post, non, inter, mono, sup.
8. Mark diacritically and divide into syllables the following, and name the sign that indicates the sound: card, ball, mercy, sir, odd, cell, rise, blood, fare, last.
9. Use the following correctly in sentences: cite, site, sight, fane, fain, feign, vane, vain, vein, raze, raise, rays.
10. Write 10 words frequently mispronounced and indicate pronunciation by use of diacritical marks and by syllabication.

GEOGRAPHY (Time, 1 hour)

1. What is climate? Upon what does climate depend?
2. How do you account for the extremes of climate in Kansas?
3. Of what use are rivers? Of what use is the ocean?
4. Describe the mountains of North America.
5. Name and describe the following: Monrovia, Odessa, Denver, Manitoba, Hecla, Yukon, St. Helena, Juan Fernandez, Aspinwall, and Orinoco.
6. Name and locate the principal trade centers of the US. Name all the republics of Europe and give the capital of each.
7. Why is the Atlantic Coast colder than the Pacific in the same latitude?
8. Describe the process by which the water of the ocean returns to the sources of rivers.
9. Describe the movements of the earth. Give the inclination of the earth.

I won't ask how you did.

Average Americans today no longer end our education after the eighth grade. Like many industrialized countries, the vast majority of our citizens have completed secondary education, and a rising number of college graduates outnumbers high school dropouts. Sounds great. But are we any smarter? Are our college degrees worth anywhere close to the tens—sometimes hundreds—of thousands of dollars we're paying for them?

General Jim Mattis, who served as America's twenty-sixth secretary of defense, has noted in his own book that "if you haven't read hundreds of books, you are functionally illiterate, and you will be incompetent, because your personal experiences alone aren't broad enough to sustain you."[37]

He is hitting on a basic truth—personal experiences alone are not sufficient for developing an expansive, competent understanding of the world. Reading widely exposes us to diverse perspectives, historical contexts, and complex problem-solving scenarios that we may not otherwise encounter in our own lives.

Reading and building on historical, societal, or otherwise external knowledge allows us to stand on the proverbial shoulders of giants. By engaging with the accumulated wisdom and experiences of others, we gain insights that enrich our own understanding of the world. In addition to helping us avoid past mistakes and replicate successful strategies, exposure to diverse ideas and viewpoints fosters creativity and innovation, as new ideas often emerge from synthesizing existing knowledge in novel ways. Reading broadens our intellectual horizon, providing a richer foundation for thought and action in all situations.

So how is our literacy?

In 1890, with a significant percentage of our population having previously been enslaved, 13 percent of the US population was illiterate. Today, with slavery well in our past, that number rests at 21 percent—and that's just for adults. But it gets worse. According to a 2020 Department of Education report, 54 percent of US adults have English prose literacy below a sixth-grade level. Let me translate that for you: Over half of Americans aren't reading much of anything beyond social media snippets because they can't do it at a high functioning level. In short, over half of America is functionally illiterate.

Sure, we know things that our recent ancestors didn't. But that's not what matters. Albert Einstein emphasized that education is not the learning of facts, but the training of the mind to think. This was supposed to be the entire point of our lifelong studies. Do we even understand how to approach the process of thinking today? Are we teaching our youth?

When you hear people colloquially speak of the importance of learning *how* to think, rather than *what* to think, they're referring (whether they realize it or not) to first-principles thinking, an approach used by philosophers, Nobel Prize winners, entrepreneurs, and successful humans of all ilk throughout history. As discussed in the previous chapter, it was employed routinely by America's Founders. Sadly, this basic skill is rarely taught by today's educational institutions, let alone employed effectively.

First-principles thinking is a disciplined approach to analysis and problem-solving. The idea is simple: question everything. Strip any concept down to the smallest known truth that can't be dissected any further and doesn't require any assumptions to make it true. Then begin building up again from there. These smallest foundational elements of truth are known as first principles—hence, the name.

The idea was first articulated by Aristotle, the great philosopher and student of Plato. Aristotle was what we would today call a polymath, meaning that he had wide-ranging, extensive knowledge in a great many areas of sciences and humanities.

Aristotle's methodology, using what he articulated as "the first basis from which a thing is known,"[38] is ideal for complex problems or scenarios where creativity is required to reach a new conclusion. This type of reasoning stands in stark opposition to the way we normally think, which is reasoning by analogy. Reasoning by analogy allows us to draw quick conclusions by our assuming many facts as true, rather than questioning them.

Foundational Wisdom

Johann Wolfgang von Goethe taught that only ignorant men raise questions that wise men answered a thousand years ago. A lesson we'd do well to finally learn.

We shouldn't ever be afraid of looking backward as we also look forward. Of welcoming the knowledge of those who came before us and the wisdom of the ages. It can only serve as higher ground from which to look out over the unexplored potential of the future. This is how we truly reach new heights and leave our minds free to imagine what comes next.

Billionaire entrepreneur Elon Musk's approach at SpaceX is a perfect example of first-principles thinking. Musk wanted to build a reusable rocket ship capable of achieving his interplanetary goals, but he didn't have the budget for it. Great creativity was required.

"I tend to approach things from a physics framework," Musk says. "Physics teaches you to reason from first principles rather than by analogy. So I said, okay, let's look at the first principles. What is a rocket made of? Aerospace-grade aluminum alloys, plus some titanium, copper, and carbon fiber. Then I asked, what is the value of those materials on the commodity market? It turned out that the materials cost of a rocket was around two percent of the typical price."[39]

Rather than accept the parts, software, and their accompanying costs that the entire industry assumed as truths, he stripped everything down to a fundamental analysis of what was needed to launch a rocket into space—the aerospace-grade alloys and materials necessary to build a rocket and their actual costs in the open market in raw form. In doing so, he not only achieved his goals within his budget, but he has revolutionized the space industry also. Musk has made previously unfathomable accomplishments realities.

While it's important for humans to engage in multiple types of thinking in various aspects of our lives, the ability to engage in first-principles thinking is essential to progress because it encourages innovative solutions by bypassing conventional wisdom and focusing on underlying truths.

Simply put, it provides a solid foundation so that we can create what's new.

Let's be honest—this is pretty commonsense stuff. You'd be hard pressed to find someone willing to argue against a thirst for knowledge, first-principles thinking, and a pursuit of wisdom. So why have we allowed these traits that are so critical to our own freedom to whittle away?

There is a pervasive fallacy that many fall victim to—especially our young. In the correct desire to look forward and "make a difference," we often find a return to historical ideals lacking in vision. And an imbibing of both historical and current external knowledge seems boring. We tend only to want the "new."

But renewing our thirst for knowledge and reclaiming our freedom aren't the goals in and of themselves. They're simply step 1—they are the requisite for the innovation that comes in step 2. Every architect knows that building to new heights first requires a solid foundation. We mustn't forget what others before us have learned, and we mustn't set aside what they have obtained at great cost. We must not forget to build a solid foundation for ourselves and our societies.

Sovereign individuals build a solid foundation for themselves and their communities so that they can be free to create what's next. And there's nothing boring about what's next.

CHAPTER FIVE | **GLOBALISM**

The road to hell is paved with good intentions.

—a proverb

GLOBALISM | A LONG WAY FROM THE INDIVIDUAL

Virtually all the earth is divided into parts by invisible, sometimes arbitrary lines that we call borders. This is true whether the sovereign state within those borders is governed by a liberal constitution, a theocracy, a communist regime, a military dictatorship, or another form of government. It's undeniable that sovereign statehood is the most universally accepted political form throughout history.

Sovereign nation states and their accompanying national sovereignty have become the norm. These are characterized by a defined sovereign territory that houses a permanent population (citizens) and a sense of national identity, which is often based on common language, culture, history, and values. Depending on your point of view, this tribalism either fosters a sense of unity and belonging among the nation's citizens or prevents them from understanding themselves as part of a broader whole on the world stage.

For many decades now, thought leaders and statesmen of all parties have echoed a similar sentiment to Harvard professor Daniel Bell, who said that individual sovereign nations are "too big for the small problems and too small for the big problems."[40]

Enter the age of globalism.

To understand where we are today—and how and why our forms of governance are changing—let's briefly shift our gaze to the concepts of nation states and national sovereignty, their evolution, and their impending demise.

The first humans had no governments to contend with. Humanity in its natural state was truly sovereign. Over the millennia, we have either submitted to or voluntarily assumed a myriad of governments, religions, and ideologies—only to throw them off and try again. Former US senator and president of the World Federalist Association Alan Cranston once noted, "Civilizations rose and fell, but through it all, issues of sovereignty—who was in charge and who wasn't—largely told the tale."[41]

City-states, such as Athens and later Florence, were the precursors to today's nation-states. Conflicts between city-states led to conquests of ever-larger territories. These territories were often presided over by rulers who came to be known as "sovereigns." Many of these rulers sought to enhance the legitimacy of their limitless authority over their subjects by asserting that they ruled by a divine right, a right bestowed upon them by God. Thus, they were blessed with "sovereign immunity," a doctrine of privilege that put them above the law. After all, were they to remain under—i.e., subject to—the law, like their *subjects* were, would mean they could have been punished for their savage acts—some of which were incomprehensibly savage. This bastardized form of sovereignty belonged to individuals, but only to the privileged few who inherited it by birth or outright seized it.[42]

The origins of modern sovereign states date back to the 1648 Treaty of Westphalia, which ended Europe's Thirty Years' War—a tumultuous period, partially ignited by the tinder of religious fervor (thanks to Martin Luther in the previous century) and the ambition of princes. These forces worked together to ensnare the continent in a maelstrom of religious and territorial disputes, eventually redrawing its maps and deeply scarring its soul.

The Treaty of Westphalia, in its essence, was not a singular document but a collection of peace agreements, notably the Peace of Münster and the Peace of Osnabrück. These accords were the fruit of protracted negotiations, compromise, and conciliation. According to German philosopher Volker Gerhardt, "This was not a Church Council, nor an Imperial Diet, but a meeting of independent territorial and political entities, where, for the first time, relevant alliances were taken into account. The Holy See was present only as an observer."[43] Although there was no official declaration of sovereignty or a system of sovereign states, the royal rulers of Europe's roughly three hundred kingdoms, principalities, and baronies clearly recognized the absolute unfettered authority of each within his own realm.

Under the auspices of this treaty, the tempest of religious wars was quelled, allowing the principle of *cuius regio, eius religio* (a Latin phrase which literally means "whose realm, their religion") to be reaffirmed, granting rulers the authority to determine the religious denomination of their own realms. This marked a significant stride toward religious tolerance, a concept that was beginning to take root in the consciousness of Europe.

While there is much debate between structuralists and those claiming the power of ideas as the revolutionary fuel leading to Westphalia, there is no such debate that in its wake, states were the chief form of constitutional authority in Europe and faced no serious rival from the Holy Roman Empire.

The best way to understand the critical importance of Westphalia to international relations is by comparison with the political and cultural environment preceding the treaty—Europe was experiencing its peak, the high Middle Ages. During this time, all of society was united in a collectivist union, similar to how the church was also seen as united, in the body of Christ. There was no sovereignty, no supreme authority. Sure, the pope and emperor intervened regularly in the affairs of kings, nobles, and other authorities, but those same kings, nobles, and authorities, similarly, held certain privileges of their own. (Simply calling a leader *sovereign* didn't mean they were.)

In addition to the collectivist union in *attitude*, there was also no sovereign state requirement of territory met, as *Respublica Christiana*[44]—the idea of being one unified Christian community—encompassed all Western Christians, whether in Europe or abroad. In short, the Middle Ages at its height was markedly without sovereignty.

Only in the later centuries of the Middle Ages did the landscape begin to sprout sovereign states. By the eve of the Reformation in 1517, monarchs in Britain, France, and Sweden had established supremacy over the church and other rival powers. And a small system of Italian sovereign states had survived for over a century, thanks to natural Alpine protection and isolation from Europe.

But Europe's path to sovereignty was far from easy. Also in 1517, Charles V, head of the Hapsburg family and a Catholic, ascended to the Spanish throne, where he not only ruled Castile, Aragon, and the Netherlands but also parts of Italy, Burgundy, and Austria—his inheritance from his grandparents. He became Holy Roman Emperor in 1519, expanding his authority across Germany, Switzerland, and other regions in Italy and the Netherlands, and shortly afterward added the crowns of Bohemia, Croatia, and Hungary. When his Spanish army attacked Rome in 1527, the Italian states system imploded.

Charles V was emperor and commander of the Catholic armies. Yet even he was truly sovereign only in Spain. Other territories, such as the Netherlands and Germany, had rights and privileges that pre-dated and limited his rule.

When Charles V abdicated in 1555–56, his successor, Philip II, the new king of Spain, failed to be elected emperor and, thus, lost his title to Austria and Germany. Sovereignty continued to make gains throughout the continent during this period, and in 1581, the northern provinces of the Netherlands declared independence from Spain—resulting in nearly seven decades of fighting (leading all the way to 1648). Meanwhile, the religious wars of Protestantism and the Counter Reformation (a revival of Catholicism advocating for a restored power and influence of the church spanning Christendom) raged on—ultimately, culminating in the Thirty Years' War.

Thus, the Treaty of Westphalia is enshrined as a seminal moment, signaling the end of one era and the dawn of another and bringing Europe from the medieval world to the modern international system.[45] The classic statement to this effect comes from a 1948 article by international lawyer Leo Gross, who calls the settlement, "the majestic portal which leads from the old world into the new world."[46] Mankind heralded this new era, where diplomacy and dialogue would prevail over the discord of arms.

But of course, as it always does, war and discord did come over the ensuing centuries—often in the form of internal revolutions. America's founding fathers, as we have seen, opted for a sharp deviation from their brethren around the world. As Yale professor Edward S. Morgan has wittily remarked, Americans replaced a government that was over them with a government that was under them. They did so by recognizing the eternal truth of what Thomas Jefferson termed "the Laws of Nature and of Nature's God."[47] Personal sovereignty.

Yet in an enlightened era, where rebels threw off royal rule in favor of nation states, America remained unique in her ideals of personal sovereignty.

It's the French who redirected the world back to the Westphalian notions of sovereign states—this time with a new twist. The French Revolution set forth a new concept in sovereignty, one in which sovereignty belonged to nations. This was different than the sovereignty of rulers and their dynasties (leaders known as "sovereigns," or as possessing "sovereign immunity") and different than the sovereignty of individuals whose government served them, as in America (known as "personal sovereignty"). France's Declaration of the Rights of Man and of the Citizen established the idea that sovereignty resides in the nation as a whole and its collective will. This concept has remained with France throughout her constitutional iterations, likely best captured in the language of the 1958 Constitution of the French Fifth Republic: "Sovereignty is one, indivisible, unalienable and imprescriptible; it belongs to the Nation; no group can attribute sovereignty to itself, nor can any individual arrogate it to himself."[48]

National sovereignty.

France's concept of collective national sovereignty remains forever entangled with our modern-day democratic nation-states. Today, when world leaders espouse "democratic rights and freedoms," they are speaking of this collectivist form of national sovereignty, wherein sovereignty rests with a nation, and its citizens have a say in their governance.

Don't be fooled. This is a far cry from our American system of governance. A far cry from liberty.

ONE WORLD GOVERNMENT | AND SO IT BEGINS

The narrative history of the United Nations and modern international relations is a continuation of the quest for lasting peace and the triumph of diplomacy over arms. At least, that's the charitable version. The narrative begins with the League of Nations, an organization founded in 1920 in the aftermath of WWI. First proposed by US President Woodrow Wilson, the League was part of his Fourteen Points plan for peace, which he presented to Congress in 1918, and which required extensive regulation and enforcement. Despite Wilson's fervor and international support, it faced significant headwinds here at home. Opposition leaders voiced concerns over the cost, the consequences of further entanglement in European affairs, and a reduction in the US's ability to defend its own interests. Sound familiar?

The League of Nations came into being at the Paris Peace Conference in 1919, which led to the Treaty of Versailles. The League's covenant was incorporated into the Treaty of Versailles and other peace treaties with the Central Powers. Formally established on January 10, 1920, and headquartered in Geneva, Switzerland, the League touted an aim to promote disarmament, prevent war through collective security, settle disputes between countries through negotiation and arbitration, and improve global welfare. Despite Wilson's being a key proponent, the United States never ratified the Treaty of Versailles due to its inclusion of the League and, thus, never joined. In 1920, Warren Harding was elected president on a platform opposing the League of Nations.

We the Peoples

"We the People" are the opening words to America's constitution.

In an inversion of the American principle of individual sovereignty and as the foundational document for globalism and international collectivism (while seeking public perception that the UN was based on the same American principles), the UN Charter begins with "We the Peoples."

One letter changes everything.

In the midst of WWII, the Allied powers sought a new framework for international cooperation, and US President Franklin D. Roosevelt envisioned himself succeeding where Wilson had failed. This led to the signing of the Atlantic Charter, outlining a vision for a post-war world, by President Roosevelt and British Prime Minister Winston Churchill in August 1941. The Declaration by United Nations followed on January 1, 1942, with twenty-six nations, including the United States, pledging to fight the Axis powers; this laid the groundwork for a new international body. From April 25 to June 26, 1945, the US played host to the United Nations Conference on International Organization (better known simply as the San Francisco Conference). And on October 24, 1945, after the San Francisco Conference, the United Nations—the UN—was officially established, with the ratification of its charter by fifty countries, including the major Allied powers. The same sovereignty concerns raised in 1918 were voiced once again, but America had decisively emerged as the victor of WWII, and this time the president wasn't going to be denied. The new inter-governmental organization would forever change the course of history.

The UN Charter grants the organization a unique legal status that, along with the ramifications, is worth pointing out. This status is called legal personality, and it enables the organization to act independently of its member states. As a legal personality, it can enter into treaties, sue and be sued, and own property, not to mention enjoy numerous privileges and immunities. The UN is protected from being sued in national courts unless it consents, its premises cannot be entered without its consent, it and its assets are exempt from direct taxation and customs duties, and its officials are immune from legal processes for acts performed in their official capacity.[49]

Not bad for a group that no one elected. But we're not done.

Under Chapter VII of the UN Charter, the Security Council has the authority to make decisions that are binding on all member states. This includes measures for maintaining or restoring international peace and security, such as sanctions or military interventions. Member states are obligated to comply with these resolutions, giving this non-elected entity a powerful enforcement tool.

Article 103 of the UN Charter states that in the event of a conflict between the obligations of UN member states under the Charter and their obligations under any other international agreement, their obligations under the Charter shall prevail. This establishes the Charter as the supreme legal instrument in international relations for member states. So that's fun.

As the UN began its operations, it became clear that it had usurped the role of the beleaguered League of Nations. The final assembly of the League, held April 8–18, 1946, in Geneva, Switzerland, addressed the process of dissolution and the transfer of its assets and responsibilities to the UN. Formal dissolution at its final assembly on April 20, 1946, marked the end of the League's twenty-six-year failed experiment.[50]

Here's where it gets interesting. The UN Charter further provides for the creation of specialized agencies and affiliated organizations, each with its own legal status and international legal personality. Just to give you a sense of the scale and power we're talking about, one such agency is the World Health Organization (WHO). During the 1945 San Francisco Conference, the UN Economic and Social

Council (ECOSOC) was tasked with drafting a constitution for a new health organization. The previous League of Nations Health Organization (LNHO) and other pre-existing international health bodies had failed. But instead of stopping to question whether these failures were perhaps indicative of a deeper issue, the bureaucrats did what bureaucrats do: They created a commission to oversee the transition from existing health organizations to the new WHO—creating a bigger, stronger entity with its own constitution. Its ratification by sixty-one countries occurred only a few months later at the International Health Conference held in New York in 1946.

The organization intended to both celebrate and secure lasting peace among sovereign nation-states, yet it has done the most to erode national sovereignty, and following closely, the personal sovereignty of citizens everywhere. Unhealthy power dynamics, empowerment of unelected officials, bureaucracy, and inefficiency are just a few of the sirens that go off in the minds of liberty-loving individuals everywhere. I trust that you are hearing those same sirens as you read this.

If it feels to you as if our forms of government are different than just a generation or two ago, it's because they are. The world's largest inter-governmental organization also created a formal recognition of *non*-governmental organizations (NGOs) and provided a legal framework for their engagement.

Although NGOs have existed for centuries, Article 71 of the UN Charter is the first historic legal reference, allowing ECOSOC to make suitable arrangements for consultation with NGOs: "The economic and Social Council may make suitable arrangements for consultation with non-governmental organizations which are concerned with matters within its competence. Such arrangements may be made with international organizations and, where appropriate, with national organizations after consultation with the Member of the United Nations concerned."[51]

This formal recognition has led to NGOs gaining consultative status, participating in discussions, attending conferences, and contributing to policymaking. And the mention of both national and international NGOs highlights the inclusivity and global reach envisioned for civil society's involvement[52] in the UN's work. It's no accident that—fast forward to today—NGOs run rampant as cutouts for the US State Department, agencies such as the Central Intelligence Agency (CIA), and even the US military. China is less discreet and has its own unique versions of these institutions—government organized non-governmental organizations, or GONGOs.

It's important to note here that NGOs are not the same as nonprofits. Though the terms are often used interchangeably, there are differences—particularly in their scope, focus, and operations. A nonprofit organization (NPO) is an entity that operates for a charitable, educational, scientific, religious, or other purpose that benefits the public or a specific group of people. An NGO is a type of NPO that typically has a broader operational scope, often works across borders, and has the capacity to mobilize resources and influence policies on an international level. Areas of NGO focus often include human rights, environmental issues, health, development, and democracy. (Remember that last one.)

NGOs are vital to the successful functioning of globalism. You see, globalism ran the risk of failing to address the real issues that matter to people—the quality-of-life bits that hit us directly in our faces and in our pocketbooks. The larger institutions lack the requisite mandate (and resources) to act on a global scale in such minutia. And don't think for a moment that ceding power and influence back to the "sovereign" nation-states and their elected officials was a desirable outcome. No, another solution was needed, and NGOs fit the bill perfectly.

Today, we're living in the aftermath of a Cambrian explosion of NGOs. It's estimated that over ten million NGOs are actively participating in governance around the world—sometimes overtly, sometimes not. Sure, we still elect our politicians. But it's the vast network of unelected bodies who decide who's on the ticket in the first place, spend the dollars to put them in power, and play puppet master throughout their term. Want to change things? We're told to either join an NGO and get involved to "make your voice heard" or vote and let the democratic process play out. After all, NGOs derive their legitimacy from the democratically elected leaders who continue to fund and support them. It's a charade and we all need to understand it.

Lester M. Salamon, former Director of the Center for Civil Society at Johns Hopkins University, went so far as to express the view that the NGO sector represents another way of organizing the common business of society and is as important a development in the latter part of the twentieth century as the rise of the nation-state was at the end of the nineteenth century.[53]

While I don't share Salamon's admiration of NGOs, it's difficult to argue with the sentiment expressed in his statement. It's undeniable, the world has changed. Our forms of government have changed. Perhaps not on paper, but in practice. And in effect. It is now easy to understand the increasing frustration and outright anger that's felt worldwide as the evidence and implications of this unelected monstrosity and its omnipresent tentacles come to light.

But whose fault is it really? It's not as if they simply hid the truth from the little guy. Plans have been openly discussed and written about from day one. We allowed ourselves to be distracted elsewhere. Amused. Seduced by the opiate of the day. Our failure to jealously guard our liberty is as much to blame as the power-hungry collectivists who seek to remold society ever closer to their hearts' desire.

Neocons

Neocon, short for neoconservative, refers to a political ideology that originated in the United States during the mid-twentieth century, primarily among former liberals and social democrats who became disenchanted with the direction of liberal politics, particularly in the context of the Cold War and foreign policy.

Neoconservatives are generally characterized by

- Strong advocacy for military intervention: using military power to promote democracy and American interests abroad, favoring an assertive and interventionist foreign policy.
- Focus on national security: particularly, the importance of confronting perceived threats to US security and global influence.
- Promotion of democratic values: spreading democracy, even through force if necessary.
- Skepticism of international institutions: cautious about international organizations like the United Nations, preferring unilateral or coalition-based approaches to international problems.

Neoconservatism gained prominence in the 1970s and reached significant influence during the George W. Bush administration, especially in shaping post-9/11 foreign policy and the Iraq War. While the original neocons were disillusioned Democrats and left-leaning intellectuals, they ultimately found their ideological home in the Republican party. Today neocons exist on both sides of the aisle.

TRANSFORMING GLOBAL GOVERNANCE |
ONE PACT TO RULE THEM ALL

The system the world has been operating under since WWII is complex. It's one-part American power and global dominance, which neocons seek to preserve, and one-part international institutional entrenchment, which globalists seek to preserve. These facets are distinct, yet we often find them overlapping with aligned interests. They are two parts of the post-WWII American-led world whole.

It is no question that 2024 was a pivotal year, with more people going to the polls across the globe than ever before.[54] Roughly 49 percent of the world's population cast their vote in at least sixty-four countries, plus the European Union. Koe Ewe, a writer with *Time* magazine, says that "2024 is not just *an* election year. It's perhaps *the* election year."[55] One of the biggest items on the ticket everywhere? National sovereignty versus globalism.

Those currently at the helm know they can't risk losing control. So they attempted to take pre-emptive action. At the time of this writing, the following was in the planning stages. But in September 2024—several weeks ahead of the US elections—the United Nations gathered for its annual meeting and voted to make it reality.[56]

This year's meeting was named the Summit of the Future.[57] In the words of the UN Secretary-General: "The challenges we face can only be addressed through stronger international cooperation. The Summit of the Future in 2024 is an opportunity to agree on multilateral solutions for a better tomorrow, strengthening global governance for both present and future generations."[58] And to help give a taste of what they planned to accomplish ahead of America's pesky national election, they crafted a "Pact for the Future," a five-part plan spanning sustainable development and the financing for it, international peace and security, science, technology and innovation and digital cooperation, youth and future generations, and, of course, transforming global governance.[59]

International Institutional Entrenchment

International institutional entrenchment refers to the effort to solidify and protect the structures, rules, and influence of major international organizations and agreements—from the UN to the fruits of Bretton Woods, such as the World Bank and the IMF, which serve as the backbone to an interconnected, global order. Even some multilateral trade agreements are included in the definition, as they are designed to promote economic integration and governance on a global scale.

Globalists seek to preserve this institutional entrenchment as a means to protect the rules-based global order from disruption and push back against policies or movements that threaten to weaken or withdraw from international frameworks.

The Pact for the Future recognizes that the world is changing and that we can't continue to live under the old post-WWII order much longer. Their solution? Enhanced global governance. In other words, the exact opposite of what voters everywhere expressed in 2024. The Pact states,

> We commit to a vision of a multilateral system that is more effective and capable of delivering on its promises; just and representative; inclusive to allow for a diverse range of actors beyond States, while maintaining the intergovernmental character of the United Nations; and networked, to ensure that the multilateral system can draw together existing institutional capacities and overcome fragmentation.[60]

How do they intend to do it? As the saying goes, never let a good crisis go to waste. This is how they explain it:

> We commit to improving the international response to complex global shocks of significant scale and severity, guided by the principles of equity, solidarity, and partnership. We therefore encourage the Secretary-General to develop a set of protocols and convene and operationalize an Emergency Platform in the event of such a shock that has an impact on multiple regions of the world and requires a coherent, coordinated and multidimensional response.[61]

The plans and triggers for such an Emergency Platform are laid out in detail for us.[62]

These "global shocks" can come in different forms: geopolitical risk—which includes disruptions to global flows of goods or people and to cyberspace and global digital connectivity; a health emergency—I think we all know what that one looks like; or a major climatic event—a convenient catch-all for anything remotely climate related. For good measure, they also threw in a major event in outer space and an unforeseen black swan event. So, basically, the secretary-general can implement an Emergency Platform, along with its wide-ranging implications for anything he wishes. And while he must consult with various people and entities, the decision remains his and his alone.[63]

Recently, people have woken up to the WHO-led power grab. To watch the world's reaction to COVID-19 and the mass voluntary shedding of both personal and national sovereignty, in hindsight, is shocking. But when viewed from the standpoint of those seeking to separate individuals from their sovereignty, it is highly educational. Dare I say, successful. But now, citizens and their leaders are saying enough is enough. When the WHO sought unprecedented and unconstitutional powers over citizens in 2024, via a proposed pandemic treaty and amendments to the International Health Regulations, attorneys general of twenty-two US states stood up in opposition.[64] Shortly thereafter, at a meeting in Geneva, the measures, which included digital health passports and limitations on informed consent and the freedom of speech, movement, and privacy, failed to pass when analogous outcries were heard in other member countries.[65]

Similarly, citizens the world over have realized that it's no accident that the issues of sustainability and climate are virtually open-ended; the variables allow the powers that be to gain access to and, potentially, control over all parts of our economy and personal lives. While the UN and its non- and for-profit allies remain committed to the 2030 Agenda for Sustainable Development and, in the Pact for the Future, re-affirm to "act with urgency to realize the vision of the 2030 Agenda,"[66] many people have woken up to the understanding that it's simply a guise for redistribution and control. A massive infringement on personal sovereignty. People everywhere can appreciate and want to protect nature, and the issue is certainly one to tug on heartstrings. But taxation, regulation, and redistribution of wealth are coercive measures that do little to protect nature and all-too-often do actual harm.

In 2022, the European Commission adopted a proposal for a directive that would require corporations to conduct due diligence regarding sustainability. Known as the Corporate Sustainability Due Diligence Directive, or CS3D, it was approved on April 24, 2024, by the European Parliament and a month later on May 24 by the Council of the European Union, thereby completing the adoption process just before the EU elections in June (in yet another pre-emptive globalist power play). Europeans protested heavily during the months leading to its passage. If you have an X account, you likely saw some of the footage. Via other media outlets—not so much. Member states now have two years to transpose the Directive into national law, and one year later, the rules will start to apply to companies with a gradual three-to-five-year phase-in.[67]

This insane Directive not only holds large EU and non-EU companies alike to its ESG standards, it holds their *entire* supply chain accountable:

> The chain of activities should cover activities of a company's upstream business partners related to the production of goods or the provision of services by the company, including the design, extraction, sourcing, manufacture, transport, storage and supply of raw materials, products or parts of the products and development of the product or the service, and activities of a company's downstream business partners related to the distribution, transport and storage of the product, where the business partners carry out those activities for the company or on behalf of the company.[68]

You've got to hand it to them, they are thorough. We didn't vote for this in America. But it's here. And it's all for our benefit and protection—or so we're told. Bet you can't wait to start feeling those benefits.

Given that two of the globalist go-to issues (health and sustainability) have been exposed, my bet is they opt for door number three when a "global shock" is needed to implement an Emergency Platform: geopolitical risk. According to the handy flowchart in the UN Secretary General's vision for global cooperation, called Our Common Agenda, convening an Emergency Platform after a global shock engages member states, the UN system, international financial institutions, civil society, and the private sector.[69] Only member states qualify as having been elected by their citizens to handle a crisis. So, if you're wondering where national sovereignty comes into play, you're asking the right question.

In short, it doesn't. Hence, the transformation of global governance.

Our Common Agenda is quick to note that "the decision to convene an Emergency Platform in response to a crisis would fully respect the sovereignty, territorial integrity and political independence of the individual States."[70] So how do they have it both ways? How can a member state be at once sovereign but still subject to the Emergency Platform? Recall that members are obligated to comply with resolutions. In their own words, they plan to bypass true sovereignty with the "ability to secure commitments and hold actors to account."[71] Our Common Agenda has an entire section about obtaining commitments for financial or technical resources and the critical need of participants accepting accountability for delivering on these commitments.

In other words, elect whomever you want. Ideally, the UN would like willing partners. But if not, that's okay. They've prepared for that too. If those currently in power have already pledged the US (or other countries) to submit to UN authority and protocols to convene and operate an Emergency Platform, then your country will be held accountable to comply. Period.

National sovereignty is a nice idea, but to globalists it's an outdated one. In September 2024, globalists sought to forever change our forms of governance. They said so in both action and word. Are we listening yet?

CHAPTER SIX | THE BLOB

> *In the councils of government, we must guard*
> *against the acquisition of unwarranted influ-*
> *ence, whether sought or unsought, by the*
> *military-industrial complex. The potential*
> *for the disastrous rise of misplaced power*
> *exists and will persist.*
>
> —President Dwight D. Eisenhower

INTELLIGENCE REFORM | AND SO IT BEGINS

In the aftermath of WWII, when global changes were rampant, changes were afoot here in America at the national
level, as well. A congressional investigation concluded that
the Pearl Harbor disaster illustrated America's need for a
unified command structure and enhanced intelligence system.[72] Many, including President Truman, believed that
the surprise attack could have been avoided had we had
better intelligence sharing and coordination. The president wanted numerous military and intelligence reforms
pushed through Congress but recognized that it would

take time, and his earlier dissolution, in September 1945, of the wartime Office of Strategic Services (OSS) had left a vacuum. Thus, in the interim, he created a Central Intelligence Group (CIG) to handle leftover activities from the former OSS and screen his incoming cables.[73] The head of this new CIG tasked with coordination of intelligence activities among various government agencies was known as the Director of Central Intelligence (DCI) and reported directly to the president.[74]

In 1947, Congress passed the National Security Act, which President Truman quickly signed into law. Among other things, the Act abolished the interim CIG, established the National Security Council (NSC), and created a federalist intelligence structure with a new agency—the CIA—as an independent, central agency under the NSC. "But not a controlling one," a 2001 government document explains, "it would both rival and complement the efforts of the departmental intelligence organizations."[75] Additionally, the Act restructured the military, merging the Department of War[76] and the Department of the Navy into the National Military Establishment (later renamed the Department of Defense), and creating the US Air Force as a separate branch of the military.

The newly formed NSC guided the intelligence community by means of National Security Council Intelligence Directives (NSCIDs), the first of which established the basic responsibilities of the head of the CIA (who assumed the DCI title) and the interagency workings of the intelligence community.[77] The new DCI was expected to produce national intelligence—in other words, information relating to national security.[78] From day one, the mandate given to DCIs has been vague and contradictory. "They *could* coordinate intelligence, but they *must not* control it."[79] Clear as mud.

Since its creation, this federalist intelligence structure has rarely satisfied those occupying the Oval Office. Numerous presidents have sought to adjust the NSCIDs and, when unable to do so, have resorted to Executive Orders.

In May 2001, President George W. Bush directed the DCI to commission the first in-depth study of the American intelligence community done in three decades. The goal was to provide him with findings regarding the community's ability to respond to national security opportunities[80] and challenges of the twenty-first century. After all, Congress had created the CIA via the 1947 Act due, in large part, to a belief that Pearl Harbor could have gone quite differently had it not been for our dulled vigilance. What awaited us in this new century? Were we prepared? The study concludes with these prescient words: "Thus we are likely to live with the de-centralized intelligence system—and the impulse toward centralization—*until a crisis re-aligns* the political and bureaucratic players or compels them to cooperate in new ways"[81] (italics added).

We all know what happened later that year, on September 11, 2001.

Realignment came.

First, it came in the form of the Uniting and Strengthening America by Providing Appropriate Tools Required to

Intercept and Obstruct Terrorism Act of 2001. Mercifully, this was shortened for common parlance to the Patriot Act. As is so often the case with legislative naming, the Patriot Act was anything but patriotic, as it encompassed widespread restrictions on freedom. But even with this "win," Washington wasn't done yet.

Realignment later culminated in the Intelligence Reform and Terrorism Prevention Act of 2004, which finally achieved the centralized intelligence coordination that had long eluded American presidents, addressing decades of frustration with fragmented intelligence efforts. The 2004 Act created the position of Director of National Intelligence (DNI), responsible for setting intelligence priorities, coordinating and overseeing the activities of the entire US intelligence community in furtherance of those priorities, and serving as the principal advisor to the president, the National Security Council, and the Homeland Security Council on all intelligence matters relating to national security. Of course, this reduced the CIA DCI's authority significantly. Today, the CIA Director focuses more on managing the agency itself rather than the entire intelligence community.

DIRTY TRICKS | HERE TO PLAY (AND TO STAY)

Some of you may have noticed that Robert F. Kennedy Jr. (RFK Jr.), nephew of the late President John F. Kennedy, frequently speaks about his uncle's plans for the CIA and the era over which his father and uncle presided. This is not simply an attempt to link himself with their legacy (though I'm sure he doesn't mind when that happens). It's also a recognition that during and surrounding the time of his uncle's term was when things took a turn, the ramifications of which we're still dealing with today. RFK Jr. is teaching Americans basic history as a way of explaining the present.

Espionage is what we should expect and want intelligence agencies like the CIA to be engaging in—it's information gathering and analytics. Presidents need this information to understand what others are thinking, doing, and planning, and to understand what the ramifications of various decisions will be. Even George Washington had his Culper Spy Ring. It's necessary and is why the CIA was founded.

The Culper Spy Ring

George Washington's Culper Spy Ring was a secret network of spies during the American Revolutionary War. They gathered crucial intelligence on British troop movements and plans in New York. Their covert operations, including the use of coded messages and invisible ink, demonstrated the critical role of espionage in securing American victories and outmaneuvering the enemy, highlighting how intelligence work was vital to the war effort and national security.

But shortly after the CIA's inception, the Office of Policy Coordination (OPC), a division within the CIA, came into being. OPC didn't focus on espionage. Instead, it focused on things such as psychological warfare, paramilitary operations, and political and economic operations. In other words, overthrowing governments, fixing elections, bribing politicians, and other "dirty tricks," as RFK Jr. likes to call them.

In 1952, rather than keeping the OPC and espionage divisions separate and equal, Allen Dulles, who would later become DCI under the Eisenhower administration in 1953, oversaw the merging of the two divisions to form the Directorate of Plans. Dulles was the first civilian DCI—the previous were all former military—and he became very powerful due to President Eisenhower's heavy reliance on him. Having been a general during WWII, Eisenhower wanted to avoid war at all costs, and he saw the Agency as a means of quietly manipulating foreign affairs to achieve the desired outcome rather than the president sending troops into harm's way. Dulles, as often happens with people given power of this magnitude, ran a bit amok.

With help from the British, in 1953, the CIA put Dulles's ideas into action, instigating a coup that overthrew the democratically elected Iranian Prime Minister Mohammad Mosaddegh. The British had first sought to undermine Mosaddegh's government in 1951, when he nationalized the Iranian oil industry, removing it from the control of the British-owned Anglo-Iranian Oil Company and causing significant economic pain to the British government. Initially,

Mosaddegh had sought only to audit the British company (which is now part of British Petroleum, or BP) to verify that contracted royalties were correctly being paid to Iran and to limit the company's control over Iran's oil reserves.

Upon the British's refusal to cooperate, Iran's parliament voted to nationalize the oil industry and expel all foreign corporate representatives from the country. British Prime Minister Clement Attlee instigated a worldwide boycott of Iranian oil to apply pressure but refrained from further action. Winston Churchill, upon taking the helm after his reelection in 1951, was far more aggressive.

Churchill was eventually successful in arguing to President Eisenhower that Mosaddegh's nationalist policies risked leaning toward those of the Soviet Union. The Cold War was in full swing, and this approach resonated with the American president. Dulles was tapped to implement Operation Ajax, with the help of British Secret Intelligence Service MI6. It was a powerful example of Dulles's tool set: Misinformation was spread, unrest was fomented, and Iranian politicians, military officers, and others were bribed. The first attempt, on August 15, 1953, actually failed when Mosaddegh was tipped off, and loyalist forces arrested the coup plotters. But a second attempt, on August 19, after days of street protests and clashes, succeeded. The US chose Mosaddegh's predecessor, Shah Mohammad Reza Pahlavi. His reinstatement came with a US-backed authoritarian regime, lasting until the Iranian Revolution in 1979 and forever linking anti-American sentiment with resistance and freedom fighting. Meanwhile, Mosaddegh was arrested, tried, and placed under house arrest until his death in 1967. It was quite a display. America was here to play.

Of course, in hindsight, America wasn't right at all, and we likely got duped by the British. Not only was supporting Mosaddegh in alignment with the oft-preached American value system, but it has come to light that Mossadegh also stood up for the US. He refused to throw Americans out of his country when his advisers insisted he do so, while still banning the British.[82] He naively thought that, having started as a colonial nation, we would respect what he was doing for his people; he just didn't realize that those days of American values had come and gone. The America that ousted Mosadegh wasn't defending ideals. It was defending economic interests. And we were just getting started.

It's within this setting (along with other unsettling events of the 1950s and '60s) that RFK Jr. speaks of plans made by both his uncle and his father (Robert Kennedy, President Kennedy's attorney general) for dealing with the CIA and an intelligence community that had far too much power. In RFK Jr.'s words, the "tail was wagging the espionage division's dog."[83] Espionage clearly had become the servant of the other functions of the Directorate of Plans. His father and uncle's plan? Break them up into two separate agencies—one focusing on espionage, the other on the dirty, but sometimes requisite, psychological, paramilitary, political, and economic interference operations. This would allow the espionage agency to provide insight into the actions and ramifications of the other, rather than mere cover.

We all know what happened to President Kennedy.

Kennedy Assassination

President John F. Kennedy was assassinated by Lee Harvey Oswald on November 22, 1963, in Dallas, Texas, while riding in a motorcade. JFK's death remains shrouded in mystery, due to the government's refusal to declassify the official records. Some speculate that the lack of transparency may be due to the government's desire to prevent exposure of unrelated secrets contained within the documents. While others speculate that elements within the US government, such as the CIA or other agencies, may have been involved in JFK's assassination, having been motivated by the president's threat to entrenched interests.

POWER GRAB | IN THE NAME OF FREEDOM, OF COURSE

Those who are familiar with the workings of Washington, DC, are also, no doubt, familiar with the term "the Blob." Specifically, the Blob is composed of the Central Intelligence Agency (CIA), the State Department, and the Pentagon. The phrase was coined by Ben Rhodes, an aide to President Barack Obama. Rhodes was frustrated with the foreign policy establishment on both sides of the aisle and their usage of roughly the same playbook since the end of WWII. He originally used the term in a 2016 *New York Times* magazine profile to derisively lambaste the lawmakers' stodgy hawkishness and interventionist tactics.

The name stuck and—like anything worthy of being called a "blob"—has since taken on a life of its own.

Today, the Blob is alive and well. Thriving, in fact. Thanks in large part to its cozy and often foundational relationship with big tech[84] (the newest sovereigns) and, of course, with the NGOs who do its bidding.

Investigative journalists (a seemingly rare breed these days) like Matt Taibbi, Michael Shellenberger, Glenn Greenwald, Whitney Webb, and others have been instrumental in understanding the web being woven throughout society. Mike Benz, founder of the Foundation for Freedom Online, has focused on spearheading by the Blob *et al* of what we'll generously call the content moderation industry—a multibillion-dollar effort to censor free speech and control the thoughts and actions of people everywhere. Benz and his foundation have done a tremendous job of providing investigative reporting and in-depth education about the censorship industry, exposing the connections, creating a roadmap, and highlighting and decoding the lexicon used so effectively by the Blob and their globalist, neocon, and NGO allies.

A well-educated citizenry should regularly dive down these journalists' rabbit holes and would do well to understand what insiders call the whole of society model. Essentially, this model is based on the idea that a successful plan execution requires four categories of institutions working together: government (and inter-governmental) institutions, private sector institutions (including social platforms and for-profit mercenary firms), civil society institutions (university centers, NGOs, and NPOs), and media allies (mainstream media, "fact checkers," and others operating to pressure the private sector to take action). This conflation of public and private is typical of intelligence work through the use of what are known as cutouts or front organizations. When you hear people speaking of a particular NGO working as a cutout of the CIA or the Blob, generally, this is what they're referring to. An "independent" entity who's doing the bidding of the government.

Cutouts or Front Organizations

Cutout or front organizations are entities created to conceal the true source or nature of an operation, often for intelligence or covert purposes. They act as intermediaries and shield the people or organizations behind the scenes.

For instance, during the Cold War, the CIA funded cultural organizations and publishing houses to influence public opinion and gather intelligence. An example of an official agency often cited as a CIA cutout is the National Endowment for Democracy (NED). Though it is officially an independent NGO funded by Congress, it works closely with the CIA to promote and advance US interests.

Dirty tricks such as instigating color revolutions, fixing elections, bribing politicians, and other Blob activities are considered essential to our national interests. And we've historically had no qualms about doing it because it was happening overseas to non-Americans, and foreign citizens don't share our constitutional rights. It's okay if we bribe journalists to run certain "news" articles or force social platforms to adjust their algorithms to support the intended consequences. It's all for the greater good. It's just an evolution in US soft power. Right.

Beginning in the analog 1950s and growing substantially with the digital internet in the 1990s, we transitioned these media and soft power institutions from mere propaganda into open political advocacy abroad—all under the auspices of supporting and exporting our First Amendment free speech and other principles throughout the globe as a young internet developed.

But since 2014, things have changed, and the focus is now on censorship. It was that year that signaled an important turning point in understanding where top-down control of the internet and censorship of free speech mushroomed with American involvement in the Ukrainian coup. The US spent over $5 billion in Ukraine in the years following its independence in 1991.[85] And in 2014, the US and its Western allies supported the violent overthrow of the democratically elected (and pro-Russia) Ukrainian government and helped install an anti-Russian government. This raised concerns in Moscow that the US Navy might now be invited into the Black Sea via the critical ports of Crimea, which then prompted a pre-emptive invasion of Crimea by the Russians, followed quickly by a ceasefire, in the same year. Simultaneously, the newly installed Ukrainian government enacted laws targeting Russians in the Donbas region—essentially, outlawing their culture and relegating them to second-class citizens. This led to a civil war, wherein more than fourteen thousand citizens were killed in the ensuing Donbas fighting.

This counter-coup action in Crimea and the Donbas region happened in a way that the North Atlantic Treaty Organization (NATO) was unprepared for. It became obvious that the same social media platforms, virtual private networks (VPNs), encrypted communications, and other tools used to facilitate uprisings could easily and successfully be employed by our adversaries against US strategic interests. Just as we could create a coup in Ukraine, they could do it back to us. And it was likely only a matter of time before they did so on our own soil. So began the strategic pivot from promoting absolute online freedom to implementing control and censorship (and forcing our allies to do the same) to protect US strategic and institutional interests.

These practices further became the norm in 2016 with the UK's exit from the European Union, or Brexit, and the election of President Donald Trump. And it was this year, 2016, when things took a dark turn. A dark, inward turn.

Upon taking office, President Trump was faced with the reality of American governance—the incoming administration is responsible for selecting and/or replacing thousands of civilian federal employees. Therefore, the vast majority of the roughly three million such civilian employees of our federal government are career civil servants whom no one elected.[86] Constitutionally, this shouldn't be a big deal. A few public servants, immune from political pressure. Of course, our bloated government is nowhere near what was envisioned in the Constitution. And much has been done to secure the place of these millions of government employees and their institutions. Vast amounts of money routinely change hands between public and private sectors in support of government institutions and their NGO partners. And success in Washington, DC, often depends on subservience to the puppet masters or, at the very least, playing ball with them.

This is the real uniparty—the post-WWII American hegemony and the systemic defense of our associated "democratic institutions" (the Blob, NATO, the IMF, the World Bank, NGOs, even mainstream media are all seen as democratic institutions). It's the perpetuation of money and power—ultimately, at the expense of your liberty. Some of it is ideological. Globalists and neocons exist on both the left and the right. But some of it is purely convenience. It is folks realizing that their job, their wealth, their power only exist if the institutions they're associated with exist and maintain their controlling positions.

This, in essence, is what media personality Glenn Beck is referring to when he relays a story about a conversation he had with President George W. Bush. He has told this story often in various media, and it always has the same chilling effect. Essentially, Beck had expressed his concern about the country should President Bush not win his reelection bid. Bush told Beck not to worry about it, that *whoever* sits behind the desk in the Oval Office ultimately has to make the same decisions. While the comment was meant to assuage any concerns, Beck took it as the disturbing reality that it is: The people we elect aren't fully in charge. Most presidents learn this and happily make this trade. But, as the Blob soon found out, President Trump isn't most people.

Donald Trump saw the Blob and its uniparty as a cancer that needed to be ripped out of the American system. His promise to "drain the swamp" refers to this very thing. And it was his attempts to do so that became his true "crime." If it felt as though all the stops had been pulled out leading up to the 2024 presidential election, it's because they were. The fight Americans witnessed daily was a fight for the very survival of the post-WWII global power structure. With Donald Trump's impressive reelection and apparent mandate from the American people, he has made it clear that he intends to succeed in dethroning the uniparty this time. Buckle up.

Running the world via subversive actions and dirty tricks rather than overt military action requires pumping some agencies full of money and resources, agencies such as the US Agency for International Development (USAID), the Blob, and its NGO cutouts like the National Endowment for Democracy (NED). In short, you build your own capacity while crippling that of your adversaries. These same tactics have now been used on the US media—globalists and neocons have built up the Blob and its friends and sought to cripple their adversaries. After all, in a world where the mainstream media is both a key tool and a partner of the Blob and broader NATO intelligence community, competing voices—especially compelling ones—simply cannot be tolerated.

Censorship, like so many other aspects of our global ideological battles, relies on keywords. Russiagate—the unfounded allegations that the Kremlin may have helped get President Trump elected—made him a potential asset of a foreign adversary, and not simply an American citizen. Game on. When the allegations were proven false, the censorship machine moved on to targeting mis-, dis-, and malinformation. MDM can come from anywhere, any country, and it is seen as a threat to democratic institutions, or "democracy" as it's so often shortened to. Again, national security allows the game to be played here at home. And with the democracy predicate well-established, the professional class can play it openly.

Leading academic institutions like the Massachusetts Institute of Technology (MIT) and Harvard University have entire programs of study focusing on misinformation and MDM in general from both legal and engineering angles.

Harvard's Kennedy School of Business even published an article telling us point blank that "the field of mis- and disinformation studies is here to stay." Clearly not fans of free speech or the First Amendment, the Harvard article concludes by explaining that "Mis-/disinformation studies has made important—and much-needed—contributions, which allow us to gain a deeper understanding of our information environments and hopefully improve and reshape them, and by extension our societies, for the better. As such, the field is too big to fail—and cannot be allowed to."[87]

CHAPTER SEVEN | **CONTROL**

He who controls the money supply of a nation controls the nation.

—President James A. Garfield

FOREWARNED | AND FOREARMED

Back in 2019, American whistleblower Edward Snowden spoke with Joe Rogan[88] on Rogan's podcast about what Snowden called "turnkey tyranny"—a scenario in which the infrastructure for a totalitarian surveillance state is already in place and merely requires activation by those in power. Snowden emphasized that the extensive surveillance apparatus built by governments, especially the US, is akin to such a turnkey system, one where all the tools necessary for oppressive control are ready and waiting. The only thing needed to convert the current state into a full-fledged tyranny is for someone to "turn the key" and activate these capabilities.

Since then, we've witnessed COVID-19 and its aforementioned voluntary shedding of sovereignty, along with the birthing of mind-blowing AI. So, as you can well imagine, this concept continues to get play. The idea of the Blob and its globalist allies attempting to herd everyone into a digital cage isn't so far-fetched. Any amount of time spent watching content from the 2024 WEF meeting in Davos likely cements such convictions. If there were such a thing as a turnkey state, its final pieces are coming into being, ready to take their place.

This is why an understanding of the tools used by those opposing liberty is so critically important. As the saying goes, forewarned is forearmed.

TOOLS FOR GOOD | AND FOR EVIL

In recent decades, the pendulum of history has swung deep into "control" territory—from China's social credit system to the West's intentional destruction of private farms. Amidst this backdrop, people around the globe are using and iterating on blockchain technology to regain and preserve their sovereignty.

In December 2023, Javier Milei—a former footballer and Libertarian economist who wants to implement the free market teachings of Ludwig von Mises and Murray Rothbard—was sworn in as the newest president of Argentina. Mises and Rothbard are key figures in the Austrian School of Economics, a school of thinking that emphasizes individual choice, the self-regulating nature of free markets, and subjective value (the idea that the worth of an object can change and is determined by the individual who buys or sells it and not by the resources or labor that went into making it). Austrian School economists advocate for individual liberty and minimal government intervention and use praxeology (the study of human action) as their foundational methodology.

No matter people's thoughts on Milei's politics, his is a fascinating story. During his campaign, the country was experiencing inflation of 114 percent. Yes, you read that correctly. Milei frankly assessed the situation in a Bloomberg interview by stating, "Central banks are divided in four categories: the bad ones, like the Federal Reserve, the very bad ones, like the ones in Latin America, the horribly bad ones, and the Central Bank of Argentina."[89] His proposed solution that's propelled him into office? Close the central bank, dollarize the economy and bitcoin. It's worth pointing out that Milei understands bitcoin better than almost anyone I've ever heard—even those in the industry. This is because he and his compatriots have lived it—he's not speaking about tech, policy, or abstract philosophy. This stuff is in his soul. He's speaking about freedom.

Since taking office, President Milei has embarked on an ambitious economic reform agenda—implementing several significant changes aimed at stabilizing the country's economy, reducing government spending, and attracting foreign investment.

One of his early achievements has been delivering Argentina's first budget surplus in over a decade—made possible through drastic cuts in federal spending, the closure of state institutions, and reducing funding to provincial governments. Further austerity measures included slashing state subsidies, halving the number of government ministries, and proposing the privatization of public companies. He's also pursuing the discussed dollarization of the economy and bitcoin integration that he campaigned on.

And it's working. Inflation in Argentina is slowing—already having dropped by over 50 percent since the time of his taking office in December 2023. And it's expected to drop by another 50 percent by July 2024.[90]

Javier Milei is a student of history and economics. He understands how to use the tools of our age for good. Do we?

Fascinatingly, in blockchain—like so many other powerful technologies before it—we are confronted with a tool that can be used for maximum good or maximum evil. The devil is in the details, so to speak. And it's critical to understand these nuances. Coins and tokens don't always equate to tools for sovereignty. Oftentimes, it's the exact opposite. Let's explore two simple, ubiquitous examples: stablecoins and central bank digital currencies (CBDCs).

Stablecoins

A stablecoin is a type of cryptocurrency designed to maintain a stable value—typically by being pegged to a reserve asset (a resource like cash, government bonds, or commodities like gold). This provides the benefits of digital currency without the volatility.

Thus, a stablecoin pegged to the US dollar should = $1 for every stablecoin in circulation. In reality, the peg is often very close but not exact.

The risk of stablecoins is that the peg fails and the stablecoin becomes "de-pegged" (i.e., not so stable at all!). This can happen for a variety of reasons, including insufficient reserves, market volatility, market confidence, regulatory issues, and liquidity risks.

Some stablecoins are not backed by a reserve asset and are known as algorithmic stablecoins, meaning they use a mathematical equation to balance their value, rather than hard asset reserves. Algorithmic stablecoins, thus, face an additional risk of algorithmic failure, where their equation fails to handle certain market conditions.

STABLECOINS | THE WOLF IN SHEEP'S CLOTHING

Reading the financial news lately is like watching old Oprah episodes—"You get a stablecoin! And you get a stablecoin!" Market cap, or market capitalization, is the total value of a company's outstanding shares of stock and is calculated by multiplying the share price by the number of shares. In the context of a stablecoin, market cap refers to the total value of all such stablecoin units in circulation, which is calculated by multiplying the stablecoin's price (typically pegged to a fiat currency like the US dollar) by the number of coins in existence. The last six years have seen the stablecoin market cap grow from less than $3 billion to new highs in 2024 of $150 billion.[91]

Onchain Settlement

Onchain settlement is the finalization of a transaction directly on a blockchain, where it is permanently recorded and verified by the blockchain network.

For example, if stablecoins "settled" $1 million, it means that $1 million was successfully transacted and recorded onchain—indicating the total value of stablecoin transactions completed was $1 million.

In 2022, stablecoins settled over $11 trillion onchain. That's roughly equivalent to VISA (which settled $11.6 trillion during the same period).[92] Put another way, stablecoin settlements in 2022 dwarfed those by PayPal ($1.4 trillion)[93] and equated to 14 percent of the volume of ACH transactions,[94] or a little over 1 percent of Fedwire settlements.[95]

Fast forward to late summer of 2023: VISA found success with its pilot program[96] for cross-border settlements outside the traditional banking system in stablecoin USDC, and PayPal launched its own stablecoin, PYUSD.[97] PYUSD has been available on Venmo since September 2023, highlighting how[98] most around the world will interact with stablecoins—through a company they already know and trust and in a way that doesn't feel different than anything else they do on that company's platform, i.e., no crypto buy-in necessary.

So just why is this new financial instrument gaining this kind of traction and settling vast sums of US dollar equivalents on blockchain rails? Well, for starters, it's not so new. The most broadly used stablecoin, Tether (known by the symbol USDT), was launched in 2014. Note that Tether is not an American product, but it is pegged to the dollar because, well, a dollar is what the world needs.

In short, stablecoins are crypto that is typically pegged to another asset class (often, fiat), and the most popular are pegged to the US dollar. As a young, volatile marketplace, the need arose in the bitcoin and crypto sectors to price assets against and trade them via something that is onchain and of stable value. Stablecoins filled this need, and their value cannot be overstated. These unique digital assets further allow collateralization and non-volatile yield in decentralized finance (referred to as DeFi).

It's worth taking a moment to analyze the stablecoin business model, as it's immediately apparent why the big boys all have (or want) one. Let's take a fiat-collateralized US dollar-pegged stablecoin; these assets are typically collateralized by actual fiat currency and cash equivalents, such as treasuries. A customer sends currency, via the legacy banking system, to the stablecoin issuer, who then generates the corresponding stablecoins in exchange for the newly held collateral. The customer is then (theoretically) free to transfer and use those stablecoins wherever they wish onchain.[99] Want to cash out and go back to off-chain fiat? Simply reverse the process. Upon receipt of the stable-coins, the issuer "burns" them, deleting the tokens from its ledger, and provides the customer with the requested corre-sponding amount of fiat currency.

Stablecoin issuers make money via fees and investment of the held collateral, resulting in a very lucrative business. For example, Tether invests its reserves into a basket of cash and cash equivalents, corporate bonds, precious metals, bitcoin, secured loans, and other investments.[100] In 2023, the company reported a net profit of $6.2 billion with only sixty employees—of which approximately $4 billion repre-sented the net operating profits generated by US Treasuries, Reverse Repo, and money market funds.[101]

Stablecoins are a business. Issued by private institutions, by definition, they are centralized. And, as a side note, many are owned by folks who may not exactly be freedom-loving. For example, Circle, parent company of stablecoin USDC, is a partner organization of the WEF.[102] Stablecoins are, ultimately, just privately controlled code, which means they are programmable. The centralized issuer can, at will, freeze and unfreeze accounts, wipe an account and burn its tokens, reclaim tokens to a "rightful owner," etc. In fact, a peek into the code of many of today's stablecoins reveals exactly this. Private stablecoin issuers must already freeze accounts in response to law enforcement directives. Perhaps in the future, issuers will be required to flow through the monetary policy of the pegged fiat.

It's worth noting that, to date, many stablecoin issuers have been good actors and that the programmability feature hasn't been used to interfere with holdings. It also goes without saying that these assets aren't inherently evil just because they're not geared toward the promotion of sovereignty. That's not their role. Their function is to facilitate trade on blockchain rails, and they excel at doing just that. Stablecoin-based transacting is faster, cheaper, and can take place 24/7, anywhere at any time.

Stablecoins have also served another fascinating role, allowing anyone anywhere with a smartphone to access the US banking system—whether or not their local government allows it. Think back to Argentina and its 114 percent inflation. Prior to Milei's election, it was extremely difficult to convert pesos to physical dollars, and where possible, citizens typically paid huge markups for doing so. Deposit dollars into an Argentinian bank account and you risked confiscation. But with stablecoins, Argentinians now had a way to obtain, hold, and transact in dollars outside of the local corrupt and failing system. This innovation has been a game changer for many around the globe in similar situations.

Regulation of stablecoins is currently all over the map. But make no mistake, new rules and oversight committees are en route. If there is anything blockchain-related that keeps central bankers, governments, regulators, and those leading financial institutions around the world up at night, it's stablecoins.

Cross-Border Trade Settlement

Cross-border trade settlement refers to the process of completing a trade transaction between parties in different countries. It involves the transfer of goods or services across borders, along with the associated payment, which often requires currency exchange and compliance with international financial regulations. In short, buyers fulfill their obligations under the agreed terms, and sellers get paid. Depending on their financial strategy or needs, sellers have the flexibility to convert the received currency or hold it in reserve.

CONTROL MEETS PROGRAMMABILITY |
AN ORWELLIAN DREAM

Now let's turn to CBDCs. While most of us interact daily with fiat currencies in a digital format, it's important to recognize that the currencies themselves aren't digital. It's the interface that's digital. Central bank digital currencies, on the other hand, are true digital fiat, backed (for better or worse) by the full faith and credit of the issuing government. They are the first truly digital political, government money, just as bitcoin is the first truly digital commodity, or market money. Not all CBDCs are blockchain based, but most are. Central bankers extol the virtues of these digital instruments, telling us they'll make banking and other financial services more accessible while better arming law enforcement to detect and prevent criminal activity. The reason for both? The eventual elimination of cash.

While to many, the elimination of cash sounds like a conspiracy theory, it's really a simple requisite. Private transactions that take place with no oversight are in direct contradiction to the heavily surveilled world we increasingly find ourselves in. If you think about it from the perspective of a central banker, their job is to regulate the purchasing power of their country's currency, among other mandates. Thus, the more tools in their kit, the better. The more control, the better. Direct transparency and programmability of every issuance? Sold.

Agustin Carstens, head of the Bank for International Settlements (BIS, the central bank of central banks), has explained it thus: "For example in cash, we don't know for example who is using a hundred-dollar bill today, we don't know who is using a one-thousand-peso bill today. A key difference with a CBDC is that central bank will have absolute control on the rules and regulations that determine the use of that expression of central bank liability. And also, we will have the technology to enforce that. Those two issues are extremely important, and that makes a huge difference with respect to what cash is."[103]

Just what might central bankers be looking to enforce? Perhaps incentivizing spending over saving. Hello negative interest rates. In the IMF's own words, "in a cashless world, there is no lower bound."[104] CBDCs can even be programmed to disappear altogether if not used by a certain date. That's handy. Perhaps the desire is to define or limit the types of items that can be purchased (maybe even by income quintile). Done. Or perhaps the need of the day is for climate or racial policies to have an immediate economic impact. Done. The whims of those in power can now control your precious earnings. This is the danger (and to many, the promise) of CBDCs. And for those who think you will just choose to stay away from CBDCs, that won't be a choice if you have a bank account. One day you'll wake up, and everything digital will have converted.

Clearly CBDCs are a political minefield—both for an "independent" Federal Reserve Bank that's not officially part of the government and for the political party overseeing CBDC issuance. So why—other than the irresistible desire for control via programmable monetary (and fiscal) policy—would our Fed and its counterparts around the world be considering such tools?

The remaining answer seems to lie in trade and cross-border settlements.

A reserve currency is one held by central banks and other financial institutions to moderate the value of its own currency and to have on hand for investments, transactions, and debt obligations. A large percentage of commodities, such as oil, are priced in the reserve currency, further causing other countries to hold this currency to pay for the goods. Since the end of World War II, the US Dollar has served as the world's reserve currency and has had the privilege of being the most widely used currency for trade and other transactions.

Global Trade Swings

According to a trade map in the *Economist*, the global trade landscape experienced a significant shift between 2000 and 2020.

- **In 2000**: The US was the largest trading partner for over 80 percent of countries worldwide. China, at that time, was the top trading partner for a much smaller fraction of countries.

- **By 2020**: China had become the largest trading partner for approximately two-thirds of countries globally, surpassing the US in many regions. This change reflects China's rapid economic growth and increased integration into the global economy over the two decades.

Despite this startling reality, as of Q3 2023, over 59 percent of global reserves were held in US Dollars. Chinese Renminbi, for anyone keeping score, came in at a mere 2.37 percent.

See map at https://www.economist.com/briefing/2021/07/17 /joe-biden-is-determined-that-china-should-not-displace -america.

See also "Currency Composition of Official Foreign Exchange Reserve" at https://data.imf.org/?sk=e6a5f467-c14b-4aa8 -9f6d-5a09ec4e62a4.

The last fifty-plus years has seen the same payment rails used to transmit funds globally. Legacy systems like the Society for Worldwide Interbank Financial Telecommunications (SWIFT) have served their purpose well, but today deliver slow, expensive transactions due to the institutions' implementation of too few innovations, too late. This has been compounded by the US's weaponization of these payment rails (that it controls either directly or indirectly) against countries it is at odds with. It's easy to see why many desire new, open payment rails for cross-border settlements.

Now, with blockchain technology and the advent of CBDCs, countries have options, and they have begun to exercise them. In 2022, BIS expressed the opportunity this way: "Multiple CBDC (multi-CBDC) arrangements that directly connect jurisdictional digital currencies in a single common technical infrastructure offer significant potential to improve the current system and allow cross-border payments to be immediate, cheap and universally accessible with secure settlement. The BIS Innovation Hub Hong Kong Centre, the Hong Kong Monetary Authority, the Bank of Thailand, the Digital Currency Institute of the People's Bank of China and the Central Bank of the United Arab Emirates are working together to build such a multi-CBDC platform, known as mBridge."[105]

Make no mistake, mBridge is a game changer. A CBDC-based game changer.

China was first to market with their CBDC and has left the US and much of the West playing catch up. China's

Digital Renminbi, or DCEP (Digital Currency Electronic Payment) as it is more commonly called, began public testing in late 2019. The government rollout is continuing and, though slow, transactions have been in the trillions, and multiple use cases have been successfully tested, including the aforementioned usage of expiration dates to encourage spending, tracking of transactions, freezing and unfreezing accounts, deleting and/or updating citizens' balances, and the wholesale blocking of accounts and transactions. Turns out, DCEP does everything the Chinese Community Party (CCP) was hoping it would, and the People's Bank of China (PBOC, China's central bank) has been open about its desire to ultimately direct all its transactions through DCEP.

You can view a map and a table of the current global status of CBDCs at cbdctracker.org.[106] The number of nations where these digital currencies are being researched, proven, and even launched leaves no doubt that a CBDC is likely coming soon to a theater near you.

The rails are being laid for a new CBDC-based financial system for trade and cross-border settlements whose time hasn't yet come but whose infrastructure is critical to those at the helm. In the meantime, it is being tested and fortified in ever-increasing numbers.

REALITY | MORE COMPLICATED THAN WE CARE TO ADMIT

Something worth pondering—what role is left for banks to play in a CBDC-driven world? There seem to be two models emerging. One where banks seemingly disappear, transitioning to an almost unrecognizable state, and the other where they are front and center and hold even more power. Let's use the US as an example.

When a central bank issues currency, that currency sits as a liability on the central bank's balance sheet. This is what Mr. Carstens, head of BIS, was referring to in the bankers' desire to directly control that liability. In a CBDC scenario, as the currency is digital, there's no cash—either for you to hold privately and independently or for a bank to custody that which you're not directly holding yourself. In a CBDC scenario, you have a direct account(ing) with the issuing central bank via the act of having rights to, using, and/or transacting with it, and the central bank is the custodian. It's physically impossible for you to custody or have control over your funds. You have rights to those funds, but they are subject to the monetary policy and other laws and regulations.

So where does that leave banks? Well, have you noticed lately that the tellers at your banks are starting to disappear, and instead banks are offering (increasingly virtual) investment advising, lending, and other services? In a world where the concept of deposits has been shattered, these financial institutions would look more like service providers, albeit with continued armies of internal market strategists and traders.

The other option in play is the exact inverse of this scenario. One in which the Fed issues a CBDC, but 100 percent of that currency in circulation is allocated to banks and other regulated financial institutions or its own balance sheet—i.e., no CBDC is in private hands. Those banks would, in turn, issue stablecoins backed by their CBDCs and other holdings, and these stablecoins are what you would interact with. (And all we can do is hope the banks are honest accountants and the 1:1 peg remains.) Cash would, similarly, be phased out of existence. But now instead of having an account(ing) with the Fed, it's with your private bank of choice. Other than that, the programmability, surveillance, and loss of control and ownership rights over "your" funds remain the same.

Jerome Powell, chairman of the US Federal Reserve, recently weighed in on this topic, seemingly showing a preference for CBDC issuance to private banks who already have accounts at the Fed:

> The idea is that as technology has evolved, money has become digital. So, the thought was that the government could create a digital form of money that people could then transfer among themselves. Now, of course, that raises a concern that if that were a government account the government would see all of your transactions. And that's just something we would not stand for or do or propose here in the United States. That is how it works in China, for example. If we were ever to do something like this, and we're a very long way from even thinking about it, we would do this through the banking system. The last thing we would want, we the Federal Reserve would want, would be to have individual accounts for all Americans, or any Americans for that matter. Only

banks have accounts at the Fed. That's the way we're going to keep it."[107]

As for his statement that the Federal Reserve is "a very long way from even thinking about it," I'd point you to a press conference on June 10, 2020. With extremely low official Federal Reserve interest rate projections, Chair Powell infamously said, "We're not even thinking about thinking about raising rates."[108]

CHAPTER EIGHT | **DARKNESS**

> *I divide the world between people who believe*
> *they're God and people who know they're not.*
> *And the only people I trust are in the second*
> *category, because that is the beginning of*
> *wisdom.*
>
> —Tucker Carlson

WORDS MATTER | UNDERSTANDING THE PERVERSION

The incessant condemnation of the noncompliant is no accident. Those who loathe humanity seek to break you. To wear you down to the point where you accept your enslavement. Where you reject your own spirit, your morality, and your ethics.

The hallmark of evil is deception. The inversion of the truth.

Hating and hurting your brethren is dark. It's evil. And it's hard not to think we're witnessing a spiritual war. The tell? That which is inherently good is somehow being perverted into something that appears beneficial but is fundamentally deceptive and harmful.

In a war, one must recruit foot soldiers. This can be done by force, but a far better way is to appeal to an aspect of their nature such that they fight willingly.

One of the reasons it's so difficult to understand what's driving the world today is because we're witnessing a mix of true believers (the paternalistic and aristocratic socialists, the transhumanists, those who see themselves as a god, etc.), those seeking power and control (people driven by greed), those seeking to preserve the status quo because it's personally beneficial to them (ones who often justify their greed with extremist liberal ideology), and those who are being used, as Vladimir Lenin so artfully termed them, the "useful idiots."

Words matter. A lot. That's why we've ever-so-quietly changed the legal definition of a "vaccine,"[109] termed the January 6 protest at the Capitol an "insurrection,"[110] and designated MDM as "terrorism"—just to name a few.

Let's look at two devious examples of such word perversions, perversions that have powered some of the ideologies shaping our world and that have recruited useful idiots as willing foot soldiers. They are *fascism* and *democracy*.

Recall the Founders' control spectrum and emphasis on the *center*, rather than complete tyranny, which they placed at one end of the spectrum on the left, or complete anarchy, which they placed on the other end of the spectrum on the right. Although the Founders adamantly rejected the idea of grouping thought by political *party* but more by political control, we still reference their spectrum when speaking of today's political parties. The left tends to favor greater government control, and the right tends to favor less.

With that in mind, let's turn to *fascism*—my personal favorite of these perversions, as it's so brilliant in its simplicity.

Across the land, whether they can define fascism or not, people will argue with you until they're blue in the face that fascism is "on the right" because that's what they've been told over and over. A quick Google search even confirms their ignorance. "See! What are you, some kind of idiot? Everyone knows Fascism is a right-wing ideology. Plus, Nazis were fascists and Nazis were on the right."

And it's true—the Nazis *were* fascists.

Except, any student of history knows that fascism is, by definition, socialism. An extreme form of National Socialism, to be specific. Such governments are militaristic and tend to suppress dissent and enforce strict obedience to authority—exerting control over all aspects of society, including politics, the economy, and culture. This often involves censorship, the use of propaganda, and the suppression of individual freedoms. An additional emphasis is placed on national unity in fascistic National Socialist ideology, including a fervent patriotism and a belief in the superiority of one's nation or ethnic group.

Here's where they let your brain fill in the dirty little trick for itself . . .

Like any good lie, this one has a kernel of truth. Dating back to the early twentieth century, particularly after WWI, parties in the parliaments of Europe are typically seated such that military dictatorships (such as fascists) sit on the far right and radical revolutionaries (such as communists) sit on the far left, with everyone else filling in the center. Fascism is, in fact, "on the right" in some countries, even still today.

Yet definitionally, fascism clearly falls on the left of our control/political spectrum, as fascists exercise tyrannical government control. In truth, communism and fascism aren't opposites at all, regardless of where they're seated in European parliaments. They are two sides of the same socialist coin. Fascism is radical National Socialism, and communism is radical International Socialism.

But wasn't it clever? All they had to do was say "right" and your brain filled in the rest—reorienting the term to our societally accepted control/political spectrum. Nazi = bad. Nazi = right. Nazi = fascist. Fascist = right. Right = Conservative. Conservative = fascist. Conservative = Nazi. Conservative = bad. Boy, better not let anyone think I'm on the "right."

See how easy that was?

Now, let's turn to democracy.

The term *democracy* is used—often incorrectly—in numerous situations. We've discussed how democracy is a favorite focus of NGOs, how it's colloquially become shorthand for democratic institutions, and, of course, how what is done in the name of democracy is sacrosanct. You've likely noticed that those seeking to change our systems of voting and governance are using claims of American democracy to bolster a hyper-majoritarian outlook, while those preferring to remain true to our founding principles attempt to remind everyone that we're actually a constitutional republic for a reason.[111]

The word *democracy* derives from the ancient Greek: *demos*, meaning people, and *kratos*, meaning power or rule. To most, it's simply shorthand for the concepts of rights, ideals, and self-rule and used as a way of championing them. And it's this assumed association with classical liberal ideals that has allowed illiberal progressives to wreak havoc in its name.

Classical Liberalism

Classical liberalism is a political philosophy advocating for individual liberty, limited government, and free markets. It emphasizes the protection of natural rights, such as freedom of speech and property rights, and supports minimal state intervention in economic and personal affairs.

It is antithetical to the modern definition of a liberal as one who supports policies that are socially progressive and that promote social welfare. And it's no accident that this modern use of the word is an inversion of its true meaning.

The term *democracy* was one of the many casualties of the Progressive Era at the turn of the twentieth century. In 1905, the Intercollegiate Socialist Society (ISS) was founded in New York, and shortly thereafter, chapters were established on more than sixty college campuses across the country. Founding members included Upton Sinclair, Jack London, and Clarence Darrow. A later codirector, Harry W. Laidler, told the *New York Times* that ISS's purpose was to "throw light on the world-wide movement of industrial democracy known as socialism."[112] Their slogan? Production for use, not for profit.

While it might seem inconsistent that democracy be associated with socialism, the idea is simple: The means of production is nationalized through government expropriation, and those industries are then controlled democratically, rather than through private capitalists.

Think of democratic as a political label that defines who is allowed to use force and under what circumstances. Socialists have long argued among themselves over who should have the power over the individual. Paternalistic socialists think of themselves as benevolently exercising power over all of society and feel we should thank them for their benevolence. Then there are those known as Fabian socialists, who think that most people simply don't have what it takes to run a society, but thankfully, there's an elite group of individuals who have the character and intelligence to do so on behalf of the collective. This Fabian belief is considered aristocratic socialism, which typically evolves—or devolves—into monarchial socialism. Those attracted to democratic principles are offended by the notions of these other groups, but they remain attracted to the control socialism offers. Thus, we see democratic socialism, wherein we elect the people who have control over us, but the ensuing decisions made by those elected are for the good of society, not for individuals or the protection of our individual rights.

President Wilson, who had surrounded himself with many from the ISS movement, spoke often of democracy. Addressing Congress in 1917, toward the end of WWI, the progressive president famously said, "The world must be made safe for democracy."[113] Thanks to Wilson's and other ISS adherents' frequent referral to the US as a democracy, America began to be consistently identified that way in the press and in textbooks. In many ways, democracy became a word that allowed both the user and its listener to infer their own meanings.

Despite its wide-ranging popularity, in 1921 the ISS decided to change its name because the violence associated with the Union of Soviet Socialist Republics (USSR) was turning many off to open socialism. With America now becoming thought of as a democracy and the ISS's describing their own brand of socialism as "industrial democracy," the choice of names was clear—the ISS became the League for Industrial Democracy.

Interestingly, while democracy became a term of common parlance, the US Army felt it important to educate its soldiers as to why we aren't a democracy and why the American way of life they were fighting to defend was, in fact, a constitutional republic. The 1928 US Army

Training Manual (something I highly recommend reading in its entirety) defines a democracy and a republic thusly:

> Democracy: A government of the masses. Authority derived through mass meeting or any other form of "direct" expression. Results in mobocracy. Attitude toward property is communistic—negating property rights. Attitude toward law is that the will of the majority shall regulate, whether it be based upon deliberation or governed by passion, prejudice, and impulse, without restraint or regard to consequences. Results in demagogism, license, agitation, discontent, anarchy.

> Republic: Authority is derived through the election by the people of the public officials best fitted to represent them. Attitude toward property is respect for laws and individual rights, and a sensible economic procedure. Attitude toward law is the administration of justice in accord with fixed principles and established evidence, with a strict regard to consequences. A greater number of citizens and extent of territory may be brought within its compass. Avoids the dangerous extreme of either tyranny or mobocracy. Results in statesmanship, liberty, reason, justice, contentment, and progress.[114]

Lest you still have any doubt, the Army Training Manual continues, stating that democracy "has been repeatedly tried without success" and that our "Constitutional fathers" said "repeatedly and emphatically that they had founded a republic."[115]

The Electoral College

America's structure as a constitutional republic rather than a direct democracy prevents the potential for "tyranny of the majority."

The Electoral College is a critical part of our constitutional system. It ensures that presidential elections are not determined solely by the most populous areas, which could otherwise easily dominate national politics in a direct popular vote. By allocating electoral votes to each state based on its representation in Congress, the Electoral College requires candidates to gain widespread support across the country, balancing the influence of both populous and less populous states.

While our soldiers were schooled in American civics and classical liberal philosophy, the civilian world continued to flirt with various forms of socialism.

By the 1930s, many of the early ISS leaders had risen to prestigious positions in the press, academia, politics, and even religion.[116] But while all of these leaders had socialist training and leanings, their philosophical positions drifted apart over time. Some fell into the democratic socialist camp, while others wanted a part-socialist, part-free enterprise system. Some wanted full-on communism and international socialism, while others questioned socialism entirely and began looking back to constitutional republican principles for answers. Only one thing was a constant: The US was always referred to as a democracy.

Only a few years after WWII, a semantic change took place regarding the word *democracy*. As a euphemism for socialism, it had become so overused by democratic socialists, national socialists, and international socialists the world over that it lost much of its meaning. At the same time, people wanted to be associated with American notions of capitalism and success—not the dire circumstances associated with much of the socialist world. Thus, almost overnight, references to American democracy became seen as references to her constitutional republican ideals. It was as though there was democracy, and then there was American democracy—the latter gaining the sacrosanct status it has today. The word stuck. As did its admiration by socialists and those seeking easy access to power everywhere.

EVIL | LET'S CALL IT WHAT IT IS

Any exploration into the threads tying our world together inevitably leads to a discussion on postmodernism—the school of thought to which many of today's societal ills can be attributed.

Philosophical movements are typically characterized by their thinking regarding three main areas: metaphysics (the structure and understanding of reality), humanity (our nature and our values), and epistemology (the nature, origin, and limits of knowledge). Postmodernism bills itself as anti-philosophical, which, ironically, provides a consistent setting for its intellectual ideas. In the words of one of its leading thinkers, Michel Foucault: "It is meaningless to speak in the name of—or against—Reason, Truth, or Knowledge."[117] In short, it's an attack on all things emanating from the modern world and, in particular, the Enlightenment.

The door to postmodernism was opened by the Enlightenment itself. No secular intellectual movement is perfect, and the Enlightenment was no exception. While in this era the West came to know individual sovereignty and the ensuing political and economic advances, it also became increasingly drunk with its own discoveries—placing an increased emphasis on reason in a way that it could not defend. Scientific discoveries, too, were flourishing during this modern era (typically defined as the period from the late seventeenth century through the mid-twentieth century), and as is always the case with such advances, man began to believe himself to be god—rejecting religious beliefs and putting all faith in reason (if there was a god, he was more of a faraway architect who wasn't needed anymore). There seemed to be no end to what mankind was capable of. Yet their philosophy couldn't defend this intense reliance on reason, and deep thinkers started poking holes. Giant, gaping holes.

From 1780 to 1815, Anglo-American and Germanic cultures deviated. Anglo-American thought was heavily influenced by the Enlightenment ideals, with a continued emphasis on individual liberty, rationality, and empirical science. The Germans opted for a counter-enlightenment route, one that questioned the major themes of the Enlightenment and whose branches would ultimately lead us to postmodernism. Interestingly, while the postmodern world is unabashedly godless, in these early years it was the German philosophers who were deeply concerned by the Enlightenment's lack of place for Him.

Emmanuel Kant, in particular, was an important transitional figure, showing that reason could lead to contradictory conclusions, and thus, we could never really know reality. According to Kant, while we can experience and understand phenomena through our senses and cognitive faculties, noumena represent things as they exist beyond our sensory experience. And with noumenal reality forever closed off to reason, all rational arguments against the existence of God can be summarily dismissed. In the fight between reason and faith, Kant chose faith and sought to take reason down a few notches. In the Second Preface to his *Critique of Pure Reason*, he famously said, "I here therefore found it necessary to deny knowledge, in order to make room for faith."[118]

His thought process was brilliant. It was also just a hop, skip, and a German philosophical jump from there to questioning all objective truth. It took the postmoderns nearly two hundred years to get there, but get there they did.

From postmodernism, we get such gems as anti-realism (as opposed to natural law), linguistic social subjectivism (as opposed to reason and experience), race, sex, and class groupings (as opposed to individual sovereignty), the highlighting of conflict and oppression in humanity, equity (as opposed to equality), the continued promulgation and defense of socialism in all forms, and a kind of solidary communal collectivism. Sound familiar?

Noumena

Noumena, a concept introduced by philosopher Immanuel Kant, refer to things as they are in themselves, independent of human perception. Noumena are thinkable, as we can rationally conceive of them, but not knowable by our senses. Think God, our souls, or even something simple like knowing there's something real behind a curtain but never being able to see, perceive, or experience it with your physical senses.

The reality is this type of anti-human thinking has existed since the dawn of time. And while it's taken on many names and many forms—postmodernism included—it's fundamentally the same in its core.

There have always been those who have sought to undermine (both capital and lowercase) *logos*; to oppress, to control, to make individuals question their own worth, and, ultimately, to bring about the earthly kingdom they envision (one that they see themselves destined to rule).

I call it anti-human thinking, as it always shares three consistent traits: refusal to recognize individual sovereignty (which crushes the spirit and robs individuals of reaching their full potential in all areas of life), population control (through eugenics, abortion, or engineered consent via ideological manipulation), and aristocratic governance (seen today as aristocratic socialism, where the "capable" few control the many under the guise of working for their benefit).

This blatant disregard for humanity by those at the helm of society is anti-human. It's dark. And, frankly, it's evil and we should call it what it is.

So why do these ideas continue to resurface and dominate if they're not naturally conducive to a better human state? How have the powerful who espouse these beliefs been able to infiltrate the upper echelons of society and successfully pull the marionette strings for thousands of years? Surely, it's more than simply a case of power begets power.

Turns out, these powerful individuals often see themselves as part of a mystical elite with access to secrets, deep truths the general public isn't capable of handling (never mind understanding), and what ancient pagans used to refer to as divine magic. For the last thousand-plus years, English speakers have referred to such groups as being part of the occult, a word coming from the Latin *occultus*, meaning esoteric, hidden, and secret. It should be noted that despite its contemporary connotation, the word *occult* can but doesn't necessarily imply mystical incantations or practices. Sometimes secrets are passed down to inductees as moral, ethical, and philosophical teachings, using symbolism and allegory as the primary tools. It's about ideology, ritual, and an undying dedication to fellow members. Similar to the name the Blob, occult stuck because it was embraced by those whom it described.

Those initiated into these secret rites and mysteries believe in the spiritual realm and often credit their earthly success to their dedication to their occult ideals, often giving them names with double meanings (one for the general public and one for those in the know), such as light, goodness, divine plan, the divine, and even "God."

Throughout history, we've seen this incarnated as the Eleusinian Cult, the cult of Mithras (Mithraism), the ancient Druids, Gnosticism, the Illuminati, and Freemasonry—just to name a few.

These societies often taught that only through a person's growth in virtue and moral goodness were they made worthy to receive the secret teachings—a fact often used to justify their continued place at the helm of society. After all, as advocates of this doctrine of interdependency between morality and knowledge, their concern is merely for the improvement of mankind.

While it may seem controversial to include Freemasonry on a list of occult groups, its esoteric nature fits definitionally, as does its secret knowledge and practices, which are not openly disclosed but reserved solely for those initiated into the tradition. Freemasonry involves covert symbols, rituals, and teachings known only to its members—aspects intended to convey deep philosophical and spiritual truths.

Freemasons teach of and call upon a spiritual realm and a universal spiritual foundation—or in their view *truth*—undergirding all religions. This inclusivity is seen when

Freemasons refer to God as the Great Architect of the Universe (GAOTU), similar to the deist Supreme Being concept.[119] While described in the eighteenth and nineteenth centuries as intentionally respectful of all religions so as to unify members, the idea of universal spirituality instead of God, as understood by traditional Eastern or Western religions, became an engrained faith system of its own.[120] And as any student of religion knows, the universal spirituality idea is fundamentally rejected by all religions who acknowledge and worship a single God. It's for this very reason that many Christians, especially Orthodox Christians, have always considered Freemasonry a dangerous type of occultism: It can appear like the religion you want it to while actually subverting true religion slowly and gradually from the inside.

Occultism eventually found a powerful outlet and partnership via the UN, thanks in large part to—you guessed it—NGOs. Today, there are thousands of NGOs associated with occult spiritual practices, often espousing that a unified faith and truth undergird all religions. Those who believe we should be moving toward a singular world government typically also believe in this singular universal spirituality, hence the globalist association with Theosophy, New Age, Satanism, and even the oft-associated claims of globalism building toward Antichrist.[121]

A good example here is the Lucis Trust, founded by Alice and Foster Bailey, whose influence has been felt throughout the one-world NGO crowd. The Trust has Consultative Status with UN's ECOSOC. In their own words, the trust and its sister NGO, World Goodwill, "play an active role in the United Nations,"[122] and the activities of the trust "promote the education of the human mind towards recognition and practice of the spiritual principles and values upon which a stable and interdependent world society may be based."[123]

Many people think they know about Alice Bailey, but most of the quotes attributed to her are actually false. I'm loathe to call anything a conspiracy theory these days, so let's settle on internet clickbait. Because of that, and given her influence, it's worth a short detour to understand who Bailey really was.[124]

Born Alice Latrove Bateman in 1880, she was raised in a wealthy British setting and became increasingly upset with the social inequality she saw around her, blaming it on traditional Christianity, which she often referred to as the theology of the past. Hers was not a happy childhood, and her autobiography details her having made three attempts at suicide by the time she was fifteen years old. Unfortunately for Bailey, things didn't get better from there. After finishing school at the age of eighteen, she followed the family tradition of working for the Young Women's Christian Association (YWCA), where, despite her conflicted feelings on Christianity, she was sent to India to preach to the British troops. There she met Walter Evans, whom she later married. Despite his becoming an Episcopalian minister, he beat and abused her. Evans was an American, and upon their return from India the two settled in California and had three children. In 1915, after Evans threw her down a flight of stairs, she finally left her violent husband—a departure which was, in her mind, the final separation from both this abusive man and Christianity.

After separating from her husband, Bailey worked to support her children in Pacific Grove, California, where she was introduced to the Theosophical Society, a group of occultists whose interests extended beyond esoteric matters to the shaping and guiding of society. Upon being admitted as a member, she rose quickly through its ranks and ultimately moved to Hollywood, where she was part of the society's Krotona Colony and editor of its periodical. It's there at Krotona that she met Foster Bailey, a thirty-second degree Freemason, who would become her husband and eventually the National Secretary of the Theosophical Society. The Baileys moved to New York, where they became members of the society's Central Lodge, and remained in New York until her death in 1949.

Alice Bailey is often credited with being one of the founders of the New Age movement and is (in)famously behind the ten-point plan necessary to bring about a new world order:

1. Remove God and prayer from all schools.
2. Reduce parental authority over children.
3. Destroy the traditional family structure.
4. Ensure universal free and easy access to abortion.
5. Free people from the concept of marriage for life.
6. Establish homosexuality as an alternative lifestyle.
7. Debase art.

8. Use the media to change mindsets and alter consciousness.
9. Create a worldwide interfaith movement.
10. Endorsement of all of the above by governments as law and churches as accepted doctrine.

It should be noted that while she repeatedly discussed these ten ideas throughout her many writings, including twenty-eight books, they were never put forth as a simple list and many, if not most, of the oft-associated quotes were never actually written. That said, these ideas as promulgated by Bailey are worth understanding, as not only have they all come to fruition at this point in time, but these same threads are seen underlying communist and other socialist doctrines and training manuals for how to upend societies that honor the free and sovereign individual.

In the words of her own organization, Alice Bailey had a conviction "that the Plan for humanity requires the cooperation and service of *trained* and dedicated human beings intelligently formed about world affairs, in collaboration with those who form the spiritual Hierarchy, the inner government of the planet. Her life became an integral part of this synthesis and this realization. Without in the least losing any of her very human qualities and involvement, her soul took up its commitment to her Master, and her personality provided full cooperation in the field of her accepted service"[125] (italics added; note the desire for "trained" human beings, not educated, knowledgeable ones).

The description concludes with these words: "Towards the end of her life Alice A. Bailey somewhat reluctantly agreed to attempt her own autobiography. What finally decided her to write about her life was a letter from a friend who, she says, felt deeply that 'I would really render a service if I could show people how I became what I am from what I was. It might be useful to know how a rabid orthodox[126] Christian worker could become a well-known occult teacher.'"[127]

And just what were these occult teachings that Alice Bailey set forth as part of her soul's "commitment to her Master"? Some were of her own accord, but most, she claims, came via telepathy. For a period of roughly thirty years Bailey believed she was visited by the spirit Djual Khul, known popularly as the Tibetan, who wanted her to serve as his amanuensis. Their first book together, *Initiation: Human and Solar*, appeared in 1922.

Alice and Foster Bailey created Lucifer Publishing Company in May 1922 to publish the book and provide them with an ongoing means to distribute the teachings Alice received as part of her spiritual practices (both from the Tibetan and otherwise). And it's through this publishing company that Bailey repeatedly espoused the ten aforementioned themes. The name caused some obvious backlash, and in 1924 it became Lucis Publishing Company.

The couple had established the Lucis Trust in April 1922 in furtherance of their societal governance work, so it was a natural solution. Interestingly, both Lucis (from the Latin for light) and Lucifer were named to highlight

Lucifer's association with light and enlightenment—a connotation often found in occult practices (i.e., that Lucifer is considered the true light of the world) and fitting here in this portion of our tale about the inversion of truth. This continued association of Lucifer with light has, throughout history, allowed writers and speakers to discuss something seemingly innocuous (light and all that is good) while the true meaning remains known to insiders. It's another one of those cases of let your mind fill in the meaning for itself. All they said was *light*.

I want you to take a moment here and make sure that you yourself don't fall victim to this type of thinking. Recall our earlier discussion on civics. In discussing religion and morality, did your mind insert Christianity? Did you hear what you wanted to hear? Be vigilant. And never ascribe more to government than it requires. It's not meant to be a recipe for our lives, merely our secular governance.

CHAPTER NINE | **WAR**

We are moving towards WWIII. In my opinion, it's already underway.

—Vladimir Putin

NYET MEANS NO | SERIOUSLY

Late 2023 saw the beginnings of chaos erupting around the globe. On October 7 of that year, the terror group Hamas brutally attacked Israeli civilians in the largest Jewish massacre since WWII. Israel responded and quickly found itself embroiled in a multi-front battle. At the time of this writing, the conflicts are still ongoing and increasing. Lines are being drawn. Sides are being chosen. Setting aside any treaty-imposed obligations for a moment, World War III against a combined Russia, China, Iran, and their allies is one that some of America's most decorated generals say we can't win. One we can't afford.

Many historians have mistakenly attributed wars as the causation of the fall of great empires. But we learned in chapter 2, it's the underlying debasement of the money—and thus, the value of their societies—that inevitably happens as these wars are financed. Take heed, America.

Meanwhile, the nonsensical war in the Ukraine rages on. As previously discussed, the Russian invasion of Ukraine hardly happened in a vacuum, and the US played a heavy hand in the lead-up from 2014 onward.

For decades, Russian and Western policy leaders alike had warned that NATO expansion to the east would, shall we say, end badly. George Kennan, the intellectual architect of America's containment policy during the Cold War, stated in a 1998 *New York Times* interview about NATO's eastward moves, "I think the Russians will gradually react quite adversely and it will affect their policies. I think it is a tragic mistake."[128]

Yet press eastward we did, crossing one red line after another. In 2008, President George W. Bush actively pressed NATO to admit Ukraine and Georgia as members. It was only the reluctance of the French and German leaders that prevented membership. In his 2014 memoir, *Duty: Memoirs of a Secretary at War*, Robert M. Gates, who served as secretary of defense in both the Bush and Obama administrations, admitted that "trying to bring Georgia and Ukraine into NATO was truly overreaching." He further called it "recklessly ignoring what the Russians considered their own vital national interests."[129] Under both the Trump and Biden administrations, the US performed active integration military exercises with Ukraine and NATO, knowing full well that Ukraine joining NATO was Russia's proverbial red line.

When the dust settles, we will likely find that Ukraine was the largest CIA operation in history. In addition to the aforementioned $5 billion the US has spent there playing puppet master, our allies and other friendly NGOs have been equally active.

So what, besides the desired geopolitical outcomes, did our money buy us? The answer is deeply rooted and perhaps helps to answer the question "Why now?" regarding Russia's actions in Ukraine. After all, we're talking about a multi-decade build-up.

You've likely heard of The Great Reset—a concept espoused by the WEF and adopted by the UN, wherein political and business leaders have come together to design and engineer our future in response to the challenges of the Fourth Industrial Revolution and its technological advances. (All for our benefit, of course.) The WEF has been focused on the Fourth Industrial Revolution since 2017, when it established its Centre for the Fourth Industrial Revolution (C4IR). Today, C4IR has nineteen global centers, spanning five continents, and focusing on over seventy initiatives; these initiatives include the technology domains of AI and machine learning, autonomous systems, bioeconomy, climate and agri-tech, data economy and policy, digital inclusion, digital safety and trustworthy technology, the metaverse, quantum, and space.[130]

These Great Reset ideas and the ensuing public-private partnerships have been met with significant resistance, as freedom-loving people everywhere have innately rejected the international collectivist movement and its restraints on individual liberties. In particular, they (we) view the C4IR AI and digital technology initiatives focusing on the relationships between individuals and the state (GovTech) as totalitarian and dystopian.

While it's widely acknowledged that Ukraine is one of the most corrupt countries on the planet, what is less known is that, prior to the Russian invasion in 2022 and continuing to today, globalists and the Blob transformed Ukraine into ground zero for testing and implementing the technology being developed in furtherance of a turnkey totalitarian world, much like the one discussed by Edward Snowden and Joe Rogan.

US support for Ukraine's digital transformation began in earnest in 2014, following the political upheaval. With a goal of making Ukraine a blueprint for requiring 100 percent of government services and citizen interactions to be online and traceable (they prefer the word *transparent*), the US enlisted allies like the British government, Google, VISA, and later, the WEF. By 2016, US agency USAID was deeply involved with the Ukrainian government, developing groundbreaking GovTech, and helped to lay the groundwork for the subsequent establishment of Ukraine's Ministry of Digital Transformation in 2019, which further advanced the country's digital public infrastructure and provided a new local face for USAID's efforts.

Also joining the efforts in 2019 was USAID's public-private partnership, the Eurasia Foundation. Created in response to an initiative of the US government and awarding its first grant in 1993, the Foundation "also raises significant funds from foreign governments, private foundations, corporations, and individuals."[131] Importantly, the Eurasia Foundation plays in Russia's backyard, and the Russians don't like it (or its name).

Only a few short years after funding began, Ukraine's GovTech was launched to the general public, in 2020, as the Diia app. Today, Diia has nearly twenty million citizens on its platform utilizing well over one hundred features, including the world's first nationwide digital ID, (biometric) passports, drivers' licenses, health and vaccine records, banking records, pension assignments, state registration of real estate rights, and even housing loans for migrants.[132] These are not mere digital copies of the physical versions; everything is digitally native. Diia's ultimate goal extends beyond digitizing all government services to remote digital education and remote digital healthcare treatment and monitoring. It's billed as "the State in a smartphone."[133] One that can conveniently monitor your every activity.

Not to be forgotten is Diia City—Ukraine's e-residency program for businesses, providing a tax and legal space for their activities. Dia City currently has 1,199 residents as of this writing,[134] with another 70,000+ working for these businesses.

Throughout the conflict, support has continued pouring into Ukraine as it embraces its place as the epicenter of globalist GovTech. In May 2024, the WEF and the Ukrainian government announced the launch of a C4IR Global Government Technology Centre (GGTC) in Kyiv.[135] Only the second in the C4IR network (Berlin, Germany being the first), the Kyiv center will be of primary importance as it will itself be a working example of the technology they're seeking to implement worldwide.

Also in May 2024, at its Diia in DC event, USAID announced its intention to provide at least $650,000 to facilitate bringing the Diia app to other countries, calling it the "gold standard."[136] Estonia is first up for implementation, with many others in the queue. The Ukrainian government will receive tens to hundreds of millions of dollars for each implementation[137]—a nice reward until you consider the price of their citizens' subjugated sovereignty.

Amazingly, Ukraine's well-known government corruption isn't a hindrance to the continued funding process. Rather, it's used to tout Ukraine as the perfect locale to showcase the benefits of complete traceability. If citizen actions are captured and tracked alongside government information, well, it's all just part of the process. Part of The Great Reset.

Of course, these days, we don't hear much about The Great Reset since the campaign has been rebranded, its leaders preferring now to talk of a Great Narrative. After all, who doesn't love a good story?

Speaking of stories, every great hero needs a villain, and for Vladimir Putin's Russia that role has morphed over time with his political needs. These days, the role of villain is personified by globalism—and, more specifically, by the US-led UN and its allies like the WEF. Hence, the espoused need for Russia to liberate her people in the Ukraine from the oppressive grip of the globalist- and Blob-controlled

West, which had turned Ukraine into the poster child for its Great Reset narrative.

Taking the time to listen to Vladimir Putin in his own words reveals a man who's been rebuffed by the West one too many times. His lengthy recitations of history aren't ramblings, and they aren't an avoidance tactic. He's explaining in fascinating detail how and why he thinks the way he does, explaining his actions to any who care to take the time to understand.

Take Putin's interview with Tucker Carlson in February 2024.[138] While a great deal of time is spent discussing the five waves of NATO expansion, despite US promises to the contrary, Putin goes out of his way to prioritize the history lesson. It's not simply that Ukraine, in this mode of thinking, isn't a valid country or that it properly should belong to Russia, it's that the Russians and Ukrainians are one people. This is highlighted when Carlson asks the Russian president if he would invade Poland or have other expansionist interests across the European continent. Putin's answer: "Only in one case, if Poland attacks Russia. Why? Because we have no interest in Poland, Latvia, or anywhere else. Why would we do that? We simply don't have any interest."[139]

The potential for NATO expansion eastward and Ukraine's inclusion might have been the proverbial last straw, but first and foremost in Putin's thinking is that Ukraine (or at least portions of it) are part of Russia—not because someone drew a map that way or because the territory had been conquered at some point in history, but because the people share a culture, a language, a religion, and an overall ethos. While these reasons make for an extremely messy way to set about redrawing the world's boundaries, it's still important to acknowledge them when attempting to understand Russia's actions. NATO's interaction with Ukraine isn't merely seen as a geopolitical threat, it's turning Russia's own people against each other and using them as part of a Western globalist system that Russia doesn't agree with.

Now, add to that the continuous rebuffing of Russian overtures by the US, and the West at large—again, clearly foundational to Putin's formation and thinking as Russia's leader.

In that same interview, Putin emphasized: "I want you as an American citizen and your viewers to hear about this. The former Russian leadership assumed that the Soviet Union had ceased to exist and therefore there were no longer any ideological dividing lines. Russia even agreed voluntarily and proactively to the collapse of the Soviet Union and believed that this would be understood by the so-called civilized West as an invitation for cooperation and association. That is what Russia was expecting, both from the United States and this so-called collective West as a whole."[140]

Of course, Russia never got what she expected. While the Cold War may have ended, Russia was never really given a welcome seat at the table as part of Europe, as part of the West.

He continued to hammer on this point:

After 1991, when Russia expected that it would be welcomed into the brotherly family of civilized nations, nothing like this happened. You tricked us. I don't mean you personally when I say you. Of course I'm talking about the United States. The promise was that NATO would not expand eastward. But it happened five times. There were five waves of expansion. We tolerated all that. We were trying to persuade them. We were saying, please don't. We are as bourgeois now as you are. We are a market economy and there is no Communist Party power. Let's negotiate.

Moreover, I have also said this publicly before. There was a moment when a certain rift started growing between us. Before that, Yeltsin came to the United States. Remember, he spoke in Congress and said the good words: "God bless America." Everything he said were signals, let us in. Remember the developments in Yugoslavia before that, Yeltsin was lavished with praise. As soon as the developments in Yugoslavia started, he raised his voice in support of Serbs. And we couldn't but raise our voices for Serbs in their defense. I understand that there were complex processes underway there. I do, but Russia could not help raising its voice in support of Serbs, because Serbs are also a special and close to us nation, with Orthodox culture and so on. It's a nation that has suffered so much for generations.

Well, regardless. What is important is that Yeltsin expressed his support. What did the United States do? In violation of international law and the UN charter it started bombing Belgrade. It was the United States that let the genie out of the bottle. Moreover, when Russia protested and expressed its resentment, what was said? The UN charter and international law have become obsolete. Now everyone invokes international law, but at that time they started saying that everything was outdated. Everything had to be changed. Indeed, some things need to be changed as the balance of power has changed. It's true, but not in this manner. Yeltsin was immediately dragged through the mud, accused of alcoholism, of understanding nothing, of knowing nothing. He understood everything, I assure you.

Well, I became president in 2000. I thought, okay, the Yugoslav issue is over, but we should try to restore relations. Let's reopen the door that Russia had tried to go through. And moreover, I said it publicly, I can reiterate. At a meeting here in the Kremlin with the outgoing President Bill Clinton, right here in the next room, I said to him, I asked him, "Bill, do you think if Russia asked to join NATO, do you think it would happen?" Suddenly he said, "You know, it's interesting. I think so." But in the evening, when we met for dinner, he said, "You know, I've talked to my team, no, it's not possible now."[141]

Of course, had Russia joined NATO, it would have nullified the organization's need to exist. Something that logically should be celebrated, but in practicality is a hard no among its members.

With the West making it clear over the years that Russia isn't welcome as "one of us," Putin has become increasingly attracted to the ideas of Eurasianism, an ideology that pits Russia in a naturally antagonistic stance against the US and the West, and Traditionalism, which views the globalist West as a case of classical liberalism run amok, the result of a society based on individual sovereignty rather than collectivism.

But to understand this pivot and Vladimir Putin's plans for Russia, we must delve deeper into his world and wrestle a bit with the ideas driving Russian leadership today. Let's meet Alexander Dugin.

CHAPTER TEN | **TRADITIONALISM**

It's nothing less than the beginning of the last battle.

—Alexander Dugin

ALEXANDER DUGIN | PUTIN'S RASPUTIN

One could spend a lifetime contemplating the musings of Alexander Dugin, arguably one of the most brilliant, controversial, terrifying, and misunderstood philosophers of our generation. Rather than attempting to do that here, let us instead focus on the underlying ideas that, largely thanks to him, have found their way into Russian politics, and which play a broader role in a unipolar world threatening to break into a multipolar one.

We begin in Moscow in 1960s Russia. Yury Mamleev was an underground author and poet who achieved a sort of cult-like following for his novels and the creation of a genre that came to be known as metaphysical realism (think horror novels, but deep and subversive). An enthusiast of the occult, Mamleev's novels were dark and incendiary, and young Russian intellectuals couldn't get enough. His flat at Moscow's Yuzhinsky Pereulok, a notorious lane in central Russia, quickly became a meeting place for artists, intellectuals, and those who wished they were—a group who became known as the Yuzhinsky circle. As described in journalist Charles Clover's book *Black Wind, White Snow: The Rise of Russia's New Nationalism*, "The Yuzhinsky circle gained a reputation for Satanism, for séances, a devotion to all things esoteric—mysticism, hypnotism, Ouija boards, Sufism, trances, pentagrams and so forth—united by heavy use of alcohol in order to achieve enlightenment, among other things."[142] The group was, understandably, disparaged on all sides.

By 1974, Mamleev himself had taken leave for the US, where he taught at Cornell University and later moved to Paris before returning to his homeland in the 1990s. But throughout the 1980s, the core of the Yuzhinsky circle remained, now meeting elsewhere as his flat at Yuzhinsky had long since been demolished. While the group had undergone considerable change, the emphasis on the occult (and alcohol) remained. Mamleev's chief disciple was Evgeny "Admiral" Golovin. A sort of drunken literary genius, Golovin was obsessed with the Third Reich, seeing it as a "mystical yin to humanity's yang."[143]

Often, the meeting place was at a dacha in Moscow's suburb of Klyazma, which was owned by Sergey Zhigalkin, who published Golovin's poetry and translated the writings of German philosopher Martin Heidegger. Zhigalkin has insightfully pointed out that the mystical underground existed in odd counterpoint to the Soviet regime, "The two needed each other," Zhigalkin says. "Without the regime, there could be no underground. But they needed us too. They needed heretics."[144]

It's into this scene at Zhigalkin's dacha, sometime around 1980, that many remember meeting Alexander Dugin for the first time. Clover describes the scene:

> One evening, a young man appeared at the Klyazma dacha, brought by an acquaintance. He looked no more than 18. His head was shaved, but he had an aristocratic bearing and a quick wit. He was immediately charismatic, and came carrying a guitar. Strumming away around a bonfire in the evening sunset, he belted out a song: "Fuck the Damned Sovdep." ("The fucking end of the Sovdep / Is just around the corner / Two million in the river / Two million in the oven / Our revolvers will not misfire.") Even by the extreme tastes of the mystical underground this was borderline stuff, calling for the mass murder of the Soviet leadership and conquest of the globe by Russian legions.[145]

Thus, the event was seared into the minds of those present. The response? They fell in love with the young man.

Over the years, Alexander Dugin has evolved and outgrown his early acquaintances, along with some of their beliefs. Yet there can be no doubt that the occult, the esoteric, have left a deep imprint, remaining with him to this day.

Russian Toleration of Heretics

It's worth noting that the Russian government's tendency to tolerate heretics has often been more of a feature than a bug. At times, the government even started, infiltrated, and funded opposition parties. This allowance was, at once, an acknowledgement of a need of the people and also a way of keeping them in check. In the later democratic years, it provided a convenient narrative of choice.

To study Dugin is a fascinating exercise, as his philosophy is unlike anything discussed in the West. To understand Dugin, however, we must first understand Traditionalism.

Traditionalism in this sense is a far cry from lowercase-*t* traditionalism (adhering to doctrines and practices of a tradition) and the associated traditional values. Capital-*t* Traditionalism, also known sometimes as philosophia perennis (perennial philosophy or Perennialism), has its roots in the 1920s and 1930s but claims an ancestral heritage dating back to the Italian Renaissance.

Marsilio Ficino (1433–1499) was an important figure in the Italian Renaissance; he promoted the concept of *prisci* theology, that of the ancient theologians of pagan antiquity. Of particular focus was that of a mythic figure of antiquity, Hermes Trismegistus (Thrice-Great Hermes). Prior to Ficino's era, Hermes had ceased to have an impact on European thought due to his association with alchemy and the summoning of demons into statutes. But all that changed thanks to Gemistos Plethon, an Orthodox representative at the Council of Ferrara-Florence, who met and had a profound impact on Cosimo de' Medici, the founder of the Medici dynasty in Florence.

Plethon was secretly a neo-pagan. Another Orthodox representative at the Council relayed, "I myself heard him (Gemistos) at Florence—for he came to the Council with the Greeks—as asserting that the whole world would in a few years adopt one and the same religion, with one mind, one intelligence, one teaching. And when I asked: 'Christ's or Muhammad's?' he replied: 'Neither, but one not differing from paganism.'"[146] Modern scholars have agreed with this assessment, crediting Plethon with the belief that there was a pagan equivalent of an apostolic succession of doctrine—something that would carry forth through Ficino. Thanks to Ficino, the Traditionalist notion that there is one underlying religion "with various 'heathen' nations receiving their own salvific revelations from God"[147] entered Western thought and is the basis for the continuing occult dogma of one-world religion.

During his time in Florence, Plethon inspired Cosimo de' Medici to establish the Platonic Academy, and ultimately, the two were responsible for the Hermetic Reformation, where not only Western church teachings were reformed, but the entire city became a center for the revival and study of Hermeticism. De' Medici commissioned his personal scholar, Ficino, to translate the *Corpus Hermeticum*, a collection of writings attributed to Hermes.

Amazingly, de' Medici placed such priority on these texts that the entire works of Plato sat compiled but untranslated while Ficino focused on those of Hermes—translating as quickly as he could so that Cosimo could read them before he died.[148]

Ficino believed that the *Corpus Hermeticum* could be harmonized with Christianity and Neoplatonism and, in his own syncretistic philosophy, looked to borrow from these and other "Traditions." In the end, Ficino didn't reveal a new, enlightened religion, and the ancient theology he relied so heavily upon turned out not to be so ancient at all. Rather than being a contemporary with the earliest books of the Old Testament, the *Corpus Hermeticum* was discovered to have been written in the Christian era and, thus, was not a separate revelation, but merely a Gnostic borrowing (poorly) from Christianity.[149] Be that as it may, the twentieth-century fathers of Traditionalism used Ficino's syncretic notions to exploit a population who no longer understood where they came from.

René Guénon and Julius Evola are two pivotal figures for the contemporary Traditionalist movement, and two figures whom Alexander Dugin eagerly admits have had an outsized influence on his thinking (Evola, in particular). Both Guénon and Evola rejected Christianity and embraced pagan and esoteric traditions. Though he refers to himself as Orthodox and claims commitment to the Old Believer Sect (which split from the Orthodox Church in the 1600s), Dugin shuns all things relating to Church ideology and the practice of normal Orthodoxy, stating simply, "I think that everyone who identifies himself with Orthodoxy is Orthodox."[150]

Guénon and Evola critiqued the modern era from a Traditionalist perspective, advocating for a return to ancient spiritual and metaphysical principles they believed were lost in modernity. While Guénon's focus was more on the universal aspects of Traditionalism, Evola took a more militant and aristocratic approach that resonated deeply with a young Dugin. Dugin then blended this aristocratic, authoritarian Traditionalism with his own political and cultural ideas.

Guénon vs. Evola

René Guénon emphasized a return to Traditional metaphysical principles, focusing on spiritual transcendence and the esoteric knowledge found in ancient traditions. Julius Evola, while also advocating Traditionalism, emphasized action, heroism, and the warrior ethos, blending spiritualism with political and social activism. The key difference lies in Guénon's focus on pure spirituality and contemplation, whereas Evola advocated for an active, militant approach to reviving Traditionalism.

It's critical to understand that Dugin is first and foremost a Traditionalist. This thinking impacts both his philosophy and his geopolitics. For example, Dugin doesn't just speak about geography, it's *sacred* geography (at times, drawn from the writings of Guénon and Evola). For Dugin, the North has spiritual qualities, and often, his referral to it is in a spiritual sense rather than a mere geographic one. Take his references to Arctogaia (from *arctic* for polar regions and *gaia*, a Greek term for Mother Earth), a geopolitical and cultural idea that, for Dugin, combines elements of Eurasianism, Traditionalism, and esoteric mysticism. It's fundamentally rooted in the belief that Russia has a special mission in opposing the West.

For Dugin, Arctogaia represents a return to the sacred, primitive values that he believes have been lost in Western-dominated modernity and, thus simultaneously, a rejection of modernity and all it represents. Arctogaia is connected to the mythical northern land of Hyperborea. Originally a Greek myth, later reinterpreted by many cultures, Hyperborea (beyond the Boreas) is a mystic land in the far North of great spiritual and moral value, whose people are important and blessed. The myth resonates with Dugin due to its emphasized spiritual and cultural superiority of the North. He isn't so crass as to speak of these things as actual places. Rather, it's always as a spiritually elite people, spread everywhere and perpetually at war with the mundane, inferior people of the South (wherever they might live). Arctogaia is Dugin's Eurasia—a landmass that constitutes a culturally distinct geopolitical entity.

In 1997, Dugin published *The Foundations of Geopolitics: Russia's Geopolitical Future* and transitioned from the fringes of sectarian society to the main corridors of Russian power. Dugin understood that in the wake of the collapse of the Soviet Union, Russia was adrift, her people longing for more, and her military leadership looking for purpose. Many have speculated that *Foundations* was written with the blessing and, potentially, the support of General Igor Rodionov, the Russian Federation's Minister of Defense from 1996 to 1997.

Selling out in all four editions and heavily read by the Russian military establishment, *Foundations* shaped discussions about Russia's role in the world—both by her own people and her political rivals. This controversial and influential text presents a detailed strategy for Russia to reassert herself through geopolitics as a global power and, in particular, to counter the influence of the US and the West. The book is clear: The US and its Western allies, as embodied by NATO, are Russia's main adversaries. (Given the 1996 decision to expand NATO to include Poland, Hungary, and the Czech Republic, this assertion resonated deeply with its readers.) To weaken them, Dugin proposes alliances with France and Germany to rupture a unified Europe, supporting nationalist movements throughout the West to disrupt and destabilize, and asserting influence and control over key strategic resources and regions, including central Asia and the Middle East.

Of course, all of this is secondary to the book's main theme—the building of Eurasia as the empire Russia is destined to rule. Dugin's Eurasia includes the former Soviet states of Ukraine, Belarus, and Kazakhstan, the Eastern European nations of Serbia, Bulgaria, and Moldova, the Caucasus Region nations of Armenia, Georgia, and Azerbaijan, and the central Asian nations of Uzbekistan, Turkmenistan, Kyrgyzstan, and Tajikistan. Notice this list doesn't mirror the old Soviet Union, nor does it reflect greater expansionist ambitions into Europe. Recall Vladimir Putin's history lesson about the Russian people. Fundamentally, one people.

Dugin's seminal work builds upon the theories of the obscure and untenured British academic, Sir Halford Mackinder, who, no doubt, would be shocked to see what his life's work has come to in Dugin's hands. In a lecture first delivered to the Royal Geographical Society in 1904, Mackinder put forth that Russia, not Germany, was Britain's main strategic rival. Given the two ensuing world wars against Germany, you can guess how well his theory was received.

Mackinder's theory came to be known as geopolitics—essentially, that despite years of political, economic, and technological development, geography is and will remain the fundamental driver of world order. Geopoliticians argue that land and sea powers are destined to clash and that, ever since the Peloponnesian War, where the sea-power Athens faced off against the great land-power Spartan, every meaningful conflict has seen some iteration of land powers confronting sea powers for domination.

Taking this theory to its obvious conclusion, Russia, the world's largest land power, is fated to be in perpetual conflict with the world's dominant sea power—a mantle that has transferred from Britain to the US. Sticking to his guns, in 1919, Mackinder argued for a complete territorial buffer between Russia and Germany, justifying the need with the words: "Who rules East Europe commands the Heartland; Who rules the Heartland commands the World Island; Who rules the World Island commands the World."[151]

Those same words were uttered in a 2009 interview by Russia's Nikolay Patrushev, Chairman of Russia's Security Council.[152] It was somewhat of a dog whistle (the use of coded or suggestive language that appears normal to the majority but communicates specific things to intended audiences) and the first time that such talk of Russian empire was cited by a high-level government official. Dugin's geopolitical thinking and (neo)Eurasianism had infiltrated Russian leadership to the highest levels.

The reality is that for a host of reasons, post-communist Russia never embraced individual liberty.

While many in America and, indeed, throughout the West, argue that our form of government can work for anyone, we now know that's not entirely true. Without the personal responsibility accompanying a deep understanding of individual sovereignty required to implement and keep an American form of government, it will fail. And just as our nation is failing today for having lost this understanding, nations upon whom such form of governance is thrust without first developing these underlying qualities will, invariably, fail as well. As is the case with Alexander Dugin, personal sovereignty and classical liberalism is often, then, blamed. We're told that it just isn't for everyone. And, indeed, in the form they knew it and knew themselves, it wasn't for them.

Enter *The Fourth Political Theory*, published in Russia in 2009 and later translated into English for publication in 2012. Here, Dugin is clearly and openly influenced by the German philosopher Martin Heidegger and the French philosopher Alain de Benoist, from whose book *Against Liberalism: Towards the Fourth Political Theory* he borrows his own title.

In this overarching critique of modernity, Dugin asserts that classical liberalism, communism, and fascism have all failed to position themselves as the soul of modernity and to address the complexities of our world. Thus, a new, fourth, theory is needed.

The reader is told that history no longer has to be about progress; we can revert to that which came before. The premodern world is attractive to Traditionalist Dugin, as theology hadn't yet been disregarded (first by the later phases of the Enlightenment and then by the postmodernists who criticized it). And with a return of theology, "postmodernity (globalization, post-liberalism, and the post-industrial society) is easily recognized as 'the kingdom of the Antichrist' (or its counterparts in other religions—'Dajjal' for Muslims, 'Erev Rav' for the Jews, and 'Kali Yuga' for Hindus, and so forth). This is not simply a metaphor capable of mobilizing the masses, but a religious fact—the fact of the Apocalypse."[153]

Though at times it seemingly pains him to do so, he readily dismisses communism and fascism as outdated, discredited theories. Because they failed to create a substantial alternative to liberalism, they're not worth resurrecting. End of story.

And with liberalism no longer challenged as an ideology, it has simply become the accepted order of things. A fact. Thus, the only way for a new ideology to emerge is via dissent. In this vein, he explains that "the Fourth Political Theory is a 'crusade' against: postmodernity, the post-industrial society, liberal thought realized in practice, and globalization, as well as its logistical and technological bases."[154]

Dugin's entire focus is on setting forth a convincing alternative to liberalism and its pesky individualism, which continues to rear its head and emerge victorious over each ensuing collectivist movement that history has thrown at it; he urges, "Liberalism must be defeated and destroyed, and the individual must be thrown off his pedestal."[155]

Accepting liberalism—even sans globalism—isn't an option for Dugin, due to its fundamental recognition of the individual. And because he doesn't acknowledge the collectivism the current Western-led world order has devolved into, he attributes societal ills, such as cultural decay, spiritual emptiness, and the erosion of traditional values, to a recognition of individual sovereignty. In short, he sees individuals as having far too much autonomy and liberalism as society's allowance of the individual to become out of control and a menace to the greater collective, or the greater good.

For Dugin, the world needs something new. And Russia needs something intensely Russian. Is this accurate? No. Does it need to be? Also, no.

Part of this is philosophical, but part of it is psychological and political. Rather than delve deeper into the underlying philosophy of the West, Dugin had an innate understanding that Russia, like so many others, longed for something of her own. Something she could champion. And without it, according to Dugin, Russia faced an existential crisis: psychological and spiritual death. "If Russia chooses 'to be,' then it will automatically bring about the creation of a Fourth Political Theory. Otherwise, for Russia there remains only the choice 'not to be,' which will mean to quietly leave the historical and world stage, dissolving into a global order which is not created or governed by us."[156]

How many nations, how many citizens in such nations across the globe, can identify with this sentiment? Dugin welcomes them to come forth and establish their own empires as poles in a new multipolar world with a strong Russian empire, finally set free from Western thought and practicing an ideology of its own.

This is the real magic of Alexander Dugin—he understands that humans respond to stories and that we need to see ourselves as the protagonist of our own story: "Traditionalism offers a fictionalized account of the prehistoric past as a means of imposing a fictionalized view of the course of history on the present."[157] And Dugin is a master at weaving it into his ideology.

The problem is, he never actually proposes anything new. Anything tangible that you can wrap your arms around and get excited about. The irony is, he believes it is something to be passionate about; he tells us that champagne bottles should literally be popping upon reading such exciting text.

Dugin's proposed theory is so hollow compared to what he's clearly capable of that one wonders whether he's intentionally being vague, allowing other leaders and cultures the ability to read into it what they want to hear. Whether it's simply a vehicle for building a coalition of support for a future—and possibly a war—he feels Russia is destined to lead.

THE ENEMY OF MY ENEMY | NOT NECESSARILY MY FRIEND

Vladimir Putin's relationship with Alexander Dugin has long fascinated Western diplomats and reporters, with Dugin often referred to as "Putin's brain"[158] and "Putin's Rasputin."[159] The two men share deep intellectual curiosity and an uncanny ability to both sense and drive public perception. While there can be no doubt that Dugin is the more radical of the two, there can also be no doubt that, with each passing month, Putin seems to be moving in Dugin's direction, embracing more of Dugin's thinking. In recent years, the Russian president has moved from dog whistles craftily inserted in his speeches, beginning in 2012, to outright Traditionalist and Eurasianist thought. Is this political expediency or something deeper? It's likely a mix of both.

Dugin's most recent book, *The Great Awakening vs the Great Reset*, was published less than six months prior to Russia's invasion of Ukraine.

In it, Dugin again attributes today's societal ills to a recognition of individual sovereignty and its ensuing classical liberal ideas surrounding governance and economics. History is portrayed as one long individualist march forward ever since the wheels came off in the Middle Ages.

The Great Awakening as a resistance to the Great Reset was first coined by US media personality and host of InfoWars Alex Jones. Whether or not Jones was aware of the historical significance of the phrase when he began using it is unknown. But there can be no doubt that Dugin understands its irony within the context of his own political philosophy. He and others have latched onto it as a rallying cry for those on all sides who are beginning to stand up and say an emphatic "No!" to the globalist agenda. A spontaneous mass response.

In Dugin's words: "The Great Awakening is not about elites and intellectuals, but about the people, about the masses, about people as such. And the awakening in question is not about ideological analysis. It is a spontaneous reaction of the masses, hardly competent in philosophy, who have suddenly realized, like cattle before the slaughterhouse, that their fate has already been decided by their rulers and that there is no more room for people in the future."[160] Dark, yet quite insightful.

As part of his Great Awakening, Dugin continues to coalition build for Russia—seeking to align with people everywhere who oppose the globalists of the Great Reset. To date, he's found allies in the United States, Europe, China, Iran, and elsewhere who find themselves wary of one-world agendas. In building his ideological army, he again entices them with the concept of a multipolar world, wherein each culture can maintain its own empire. How convenient is this for China's own goals as a rising power confronting America's ruling power? How attractive is this to the Hindu Nationalism of Modi's government in India as they choose sides? Shall we mention Iran?

This coalition building is quite expedient for Vladimir Putin who, these days, could use a few friends.

It's worth noting here that Dugin is supportive of President Donald Trump as an anti-globalist, but not as an ally. In a multipolar world, one such pole would, inevitably, be ruled by America, and nationalist liberalism is far more attractive to him than an internationalist liberal world order. Bigger picture, Dugan argues that something like Trump's Make America Great Again (MAGA) platform is simply an attempt to turn the clock backwards a few steps to "good old yesterday" rather than "globalist today" and "post-humanist tomorrow."[161] And that while important as a pushback, it doesn't change the fact that until the enemy is totally and utterly defeated, there will always be idealogues looking to continue the philosophical march forward. And for Dugin, that underlying enemy is the sovereign individual.

If you're wondering why Dugin is so adamantly against individualism and even against the postmodernists who attack it, understand that he has to come to this conclusion to remain consistent with his Traditionalist beliefs. Remember, Dugin is deeply rooted in the teachings of Rene

Guénon and Julius Evola and in Traditionalism's return to spiritual and metaphysical roots. Sure, postmodernism may critique modernity, the Enlightenment, and their focus on reason, but Dugin sees the entire postmodern movement as emanating from modernity and, thus, as part of the West, antithetical to Russia, antithetical to Traditionalism, and something that must be rejected. It doesn't offer a substantive alternative rooted in Traditionalist principles.

Dugin is seeking to revive a spiritual and hierarchical worldview, which he believes is necessary to reset the world post-modernity. Even his Eurasianism is grounded in metaphysics and multipolarity, honoring civilizational identities in a way that postmodernism lacks. And while the postmodernists, too, critique liberalism and modernity, their goals differ substantially. Postmodernism's relativism undermines Dugin's reliance on Traditionalism and the importance of cultures, and postmodernism's deconstructivism doesn't need a coherent alternative in the same way that Dugin does.

And of course, let's not forget that Alexander Dugin is one of the most politically savvy individuals on the planet. Aligning with postmodernists—even when their views overlap with his own—would weaken his appeal among Traditionalists and Western conservatives, both of whom he needs.

Much of what we're witnessing today is the Blob and its globalist allies attempting to wrest control of Eurasia from Putin's Russia. This has elevated the Russian president's naturally anti-globalist voice to one of the loudest on the world stage. And to be honest, he's quite good at it. Few are better at trolling the West. It's impossible not to smile when he cleverly announces that Russia will now be offering amnesty visas to Westerners whose countries no longer share their values.[162] And it's hard not to notice that it's not the "free" West that is defending free speech these days. Just look at the arrest in 2024 of Telegram founder Pavel Durov by French authorities. Durov had long refused to censor content on his social media platform and grant backdoor technical access to the Blob. It was Vladimir Putin who advocated for his release, while the US and others in the West sat idly by—likely because they instigated the action in the first place.

Yet parallel to Putin's railing against the Blob and globalism and effectively calling out their hypocrisy, he is increasingly adopting a public stance that it's a zenith of individualism that is the cause of Western political modernity's ills. This thinking comes directly from Alexander Dugin, and it's why he matters so very much outside of philosophical and military circles. The perverse logic is that individual freedom and classical liberalism, as is the case with any philosophy, will and must be taken to its logical absolute and extreme end unless defeated (this taking to extremes is a common Russian philosophical concept). Here, that logically perfect implementation is seen as posthumanism—a danger that must be avoided at all costs.

Interestingly, posthumanism as a danger doesn't change whether one sees the issue as individualism and classical liberalism run amok or anti-human thinking and collectivism having subverted the sovereign individual and the host of other postmodern ills that we've previously discussed.

The same can be said for numerous other problems—correctly called out (if not correctly understood) by Russian thought and political leadership. This opens the door to rhetoric against the absurdities of our day, by Putin and Dugin in particular, finding acceptance with those who wouldn't otherwise agree with the underlying ideas of the speakers. And it's particularly dangerous because those naturally inclined to agree with Dugin are those who oppose globalism and the Blob. The same folks who defend individual liberty.

Remember, the enemy of your enemy isn't always your friend. After all, it's easy to identify problems (even the WEF was correct that the Fourth Industrial Revolution would bring challenges in the areas they identified). The key to identifying political friends versus foes lies in the proposed solutions.

The grave danger here is that freedom-loving people throughout the West are increasingly drawn to Russia's correct identification of the globalist West and its increasing darkness as problems, but that they don't take the time to fully understand Russia's proposed solutions. Luckily today, as throughout history, those who seek to implement their own earthly collectivist utopia can't help but tell us in detail what it looks like. It seems to be some combination of pride and assumed ignorance on the part of the general populace as easily led sheep, not worthy of any intellectual exercises, and who most likely won't take the time to read and understand their end game.

Vladimir Putin's end game remains a bit of a mystery. But Alexander Dugin is a prolific writer, intellectually honest with himself and not at all shy about the world he envisions. Thus, as Putin increasingly and publicly adopts Dugin's thinking, we can use Dugin's thinking as a guide. And his thinking sets us on a path toward something akin to feudalism.

In *The Great Awakening vs the Great Reset*,[163] Dugin lays out his vision of a collectivist future, wherein society is organized into three castes. Often using Indian terms in explaining this future, he identifies his caste system in one of the book's included Appendices, "Theoretical Principles of the Great Awakening (Based on the Fourth Political Theory)." The first caste is the "Brahmans, philosophers," whom he tells us are "the small minority of the global population that is inclined to follow philosophy, religion and theology." The "mission" for this first caste is "to satisfy the need of thinking persons—philosophers of the world—by giving them access to the real content of the spiritual tradition of different religions and different cultures. We need to promote this Traditionalist education—including metaphysics, theology, medieval tradition, as well as non-Western systems of thought." He continues, stating: "It's a kind of very special engagement for highly intellectual people. It couldn't be for the masses."

Moving on to the second caste, we meet "Kshatriyas, warriors, activists," whom he feels "should participate in a special online education program in order to create warrior knowledge—i.e., knowledge on how to fight our enemy.

To do so, they need special qualities. We should restore the values of the kinds of people who are potential heroes." This caste has "existential and metaphysical missions" to fulfill.

And finally, we come to the third caste: "Vaishyas, peasants, countrymen." All who are dedicated to the first two castes only covers a small portion of the world's population, "because the Brahmans (the thinkers, philosophers, intellectuals) are rare; and the warriors—the real heroes—are rare as well. And what to do with the huge mass of the population that is also the victim of liberals?" You're going to love this: "Peasantry is the answer." Got it? If you're not a philosopher or a warrior, you'll have a wonderful life as a peasant, engaging in agriculture in small villages.

I'll say it again: The enemy of your enemy isn't always your friend.

We must understand their end game.

Dugin and his followers are eagerly awaiting a final battle, only after which the world of post-modernity can be revealed. In his words, "There are only two parties in the world: the globalist party of the Great Reset and the anti-globalist party of the Great Awakening. And nothing in the middle. Between them there is the abyss. It wants to be filled with oceans of blood."[164]

This isn't mere political theory. It's eschatological. It's a sacred destiny. Dugin believes that Russia is a *katechon*, an Orthodox concept of the Divine Economy restraining evil, but here subverted into an occult concept of a being who is both good and bad, a restraining of Antichrist (the fulfillment of globalism) but also a preventing of the end of days (when all good things can finally manifest). Such beliefs don't usually end well.

This idea of a great—final—battle against globalists and the Blob holds attraction for many in America and the West. The destruction of globalism and the Blob is something freedom-loving individuals across the planet long for. Yet, a Russia that wants to suppress the inherent sovereignty of the individual is no friend. She's merely the enemy of your enemy.

All we have here are two collectivist movements fighting each other and none supporting individual liberty. What the secular world really needs is a reawakening to the truth of personal sovereignty.

CHAPTER ELEVEN | **SOVEREIGNTY**

> *There are no ordinary people. You have never talked to a mere mortal. Nations, cultures, arts, civilizations—these are mortal, and their life is to ours as the life of a gnat. But it is immortals whom we joke with, work with, marry, snub, and exploit—immortal horrors or everlasting splendors.*
>
> —C. S. Lewis

SOVEREIGN OR NOT | THAT IS THE QUESTION

In the secular realm, there are few things more meaningful than the concept of individual sovereignty. You are either sovereign or you aren't. From this point we can extrapolate everything else.

So, what's it going to be? It's time we decide.

Personal sovereignty—the fundamental valuing of the individual—is the basis for our freedom, and once recognized, it inevitably translates into a political system. There is no option but for all power to rest in the people once one acknowledges their inherent unalienable rights and responsibilities, their being of equal worth before their Creator.

Similarly, personal sovereignty, once recognized, inevitably translates into an economic system yielding free markets. The original name for this was *capitalism*, though most alive today understand the term capitalism as its current perversion, where free markets have been displaced by an entrenched system, controlled by the global banking cartel, and which enjoys regulatory oversight—a euphemism for political protection.

Pure capitalism, as understood and articulated best by the Austrian School of Economics, is based on the simple idea that individuals should be left free to make their own decisions about production, consumption, and trade. And similar to the civic aspects discussed in an earlier chapter, that which is required cannot be mandated in order for the system to work. Adam Smith was one of the first during the Enlightenment to articulate these principles. Many have read Smith's *The Wealth of Nations*, but few truly grasp its message because they've taken it out of context and also forgotten his previous work, *The Theory of Moral Sentiments*. Capitalism itself should never impose morality, but only a good and moral people can keep and enjoy true capitalism.

Makes a little more sense why we are where we are today, doesn't it?

Throughout history and reaching a climax today, we see the continued and concerted effort to undermine man's understanding of his place in this world. To undermine his inherent worth. His immortal soul. His sovereignty.

Without a belief in a Creator, it's very easy to chip away at the idea of sovereignty. What makes you so special, anyway? You're basically just a fancy computer. Just biological parts. Certainly, you don't come with rights.

Today, we see these fallacies playing out via villainously ignorant teachings such as Yuval Noah Harari's viral Ted talk, wherein he states,

> Many, maybe most, legal systems are based on this idea, this belief, in human rights. But human rights are just like heaven and like God. It's just a fictional story that we've invented and spread around. It may be a very nice story. It may be a very attractive story. We want to believe it. But it's just a story. It's not a reality. It is not a biological reality. Just as jellyfish and woodpeckers and ostriches have no rights, homo sapiens have no rights also. Take a human, cut him open, look inside, you find their blood and you find the heart and lungs and kidneys, but you don't find there are any rights. The only place you find rights is in the fictional stories that humans have invented and spread around.
>
> And the same thing is also true in the political field. States and nations are also, like human rights, and like God, and like heaven, they too are just stories. A mountain is a reality. You can see it, you can touch it, you can even smell it. But Israel or the United States,

they are just stories. Very powerful stories. Stories we might want to believe very much. But, still, they are just stories. You can't really see the United States. You cannot touch it. You cannot smell it.[165]

As surprising as it may seem, and for a host of different reasons, this is actually where most of the world is today. I'd like to tell you the issue is simply one of reasserting our sovereignty, but we've regressed to needing to get people to believe in it in the first place.

Many in the West have been robbed of the wisdom of the past, and trained, not educated, to value (and think in terms of) various race, sex, and class collectivist groupings rather than individual identity and autonomy. They've been exposed to anti-realism in the metaphysical realm, social subjectivism in the epistemological realm, and trained to view human nature as one of social construction and conflict. As products of postmodern education, many have been successfully separated from their families who could have countered these thoughts. The collectivism and egalitarianism they're left with goes against nature yet has been reinforced by society at large as morally good—society going so far as to publicly shame those who dare disagree.

At the same time, many in the East have simply never known this concept. Raised from birth in societies that are often extremely classist and view all rights as stemming from the government, it's easy to embrace a view that some people are just better at dealing with the world, and therefore, governance should be in their hands and remain there for the betterment of all.

The part of immigration that no one wants to talk about is that many of the brilliant folks that the West needs (and rightly wants) don't share our fundamental American view of individual sovereignty. This is having the effect of changing our country, and others throughout the West, from the inside out. While there can be no doubt that mass migration and, in many places, outright population replacement by illegals is having a tremendous negative impact on the lives of citizens throughout the Western world and needs to stop, I would argue that it's the *legal* immigration by those who don't share our fundamental values that is, ultimately, the far greater threat. After all, they are the ones who may someday sit in the seat of power at our businesses, financial institutions, and governments.

This may sound harsh. Yet the answer isn't to stop these otherwise brilliant individuals from entering. Rather, it's our obligation as citizens to make certain that we share the great insights of our civilization and ensure that our leaders value that which we hold most dear. This has nothing to do with faith (or lack thereof), as a reread of our discussion on civics should confirm.

Those working on the side of darkness understand that a world that recognizes individual sovereignty has no place for their own controlling institutions, for their collectivist power structures. Their earthly kingdom cannot be in such a world. It's why they've cleverly perverted even the concept of the individual itself, stretching it to such extremes, that instead of the simple truth that an individual is the smallest minority on the planet, endowed with unalienable rights, responsibilities, and opportunities, and perfectly unique, the meaning of the individual has become perverted. It now seems to stand for the height of personal indulgence in a way that none dare speak against, while simultaneously reclassifying the individual into collective groups based on traits: trans, black, female, and so on. It was Antone Lavey, founder of the Church of Satan and author of the Satanic Bible, who described Satanism as "indulgence instead of abstinence."[166]

Our bizarro world has come to know individualism as the height of personal indulgence thrown in our face. But we know better.

If we're being honest, they're currently winning. The world around us is reflective of the realization of collectivist goals and ideals, not those of everyday freedom-loving people. I came across a monologue from season 10 of the *X-files* (an oddly prescient show) that could easily be describing our current situation:

> . . . in a state of perpetual war. To create problem, reaction, solution scenarios to distract, enrage, and enslave American citizens at home. With tools like the Patriot Act and the National Defense Authorization Act which abridge the Constitution in the name of national security. The militarization of police force in cities across the US. The building of prison camps by the Federal Emergency Management Agency with no stated purpose. The

corporate takeover of food and agriculture, pharmaceuticals and healthcare. Even the military and clandestine agendas to fatten, dull, sicken, and control a populace already consumed by consumerism. A government that taps your phone, collects your data, and monitors your whereabouts with impunity. A government prepared to use that data against you when it strikes, and the final takeover begins.[167]

This episode aired in 2016, but it could just as easily be said by any cognizant American today. This is darkness. This is what happens when anti-human ideas take hold and grow through the institutions we've discussed.

Science Fiction

Ever notice how prescient science fiction is? It's a genre where creative imagination meets sharp awareness of human and technological possibilities. By analyzing scientific trends and social patterns, authors create stories that often predict real-world advancements, like space travel or artificial intelligence, or real-world nightmares, like control and monitoring of citizens by their governments. By exploring humanity's strengths and flaws, sci-fi reveals timeless truths, making its insights feel eerily accurate as reality catches up.

Most people alive today don't understand personal sovereignty, the fundamental, inherent value of the individual. And because they can't articulate it, never mind truly believe, collectivist control structures are viable options. Even desirable ones, as for those in the mid and lower quintiles such structures play to our base instincts to take the easy way out (at least until it's too late). And for those in the upper quintile, they play to our base instincts to play the game, go along to get along, and serve our own interests. Because most people alive today don't understand what the idea of America actually was—and still is—they look at the inversion of her ideals that today bears the same name, and they blame the few concepts they've heard of for the ills of the day.

This is the world we've allowed to come into existence.

If America's Founders got it wrong in any major way, it was in assuming that the branches of government would jealously guard their power while sovereign individuals would, likewise, guard theirs. It's hard to admit that the America—and the world—that's come to pass is of our own making. Of our own allowance. But on the flip side, it means that an informed populace who stands up for their rights can usher in an era of freedom.

It'd be one hell of a fight. But I'm beginning to like our odds.

If renewed engagement is the ticket to a better world, something very exciting started building in 2024. People began to wake up. Everywhere. Scientists. Doctors. Farmers. Engineers. Tradesmen. Moms and dads. College kids. Even media personalities. The insanity stretched so far that it touched everyone. Brought the fight to everyone's doorstep. Made it personal.

This is not a case of the masses against those in the know. The impoverished against the powerful. No. This is a case of humans everywhere—across all quintiles of society—realizing in our gut that something needs to change and that we can and must be part of that change. This is a case of principled thinkers using knowledge, wisdom, and common sense to come to the same realization. Dare I say—whether most know it or not—we're guided by natural law.

We sit at a precipitous moment, as if atop a roller coaster in that last moment of suspense before the fall. WWIII is at our doorstep—likely accompanied by civil wars within the Western world. Whatever form the ensuing escalation of conflict takes, there will be conflict. Again, we're simply at that point in history.

Which is why we must be educating ourselves and sharing that knowledge with those we care about. We must understand not just what we're intuitively fighting against, but what we're fighting for. What do we want to see, to build, and to protect on the other side? If you don't know, someone else will. And that's what the future will look like. It's critical that people everywhere use these last moments of relative peace to enlighten themselves. To dig deep. To decide. After all, the question isn't what we're going to face in the future. It's who we're going to be.

OBLIGATION | OPPORTUNITY

While it's always been recognized that individual sovereignty comes with heavy responsibility, the focus in the centuries after its discovery and early implementation were on the newfound associated rights of individuals. Enumerating and guarding them. (Or for others, pretending to guard them while in reality rebuilding collectivist power structures.)

With those principles now well established, it's time for a new generation to build upon that solid foundation—finding the strength to articulate and accept the responsibilities, the obligations, that must accompany such liberty in order for it to survive and thrive. The world today teaches that freedom is the ability to fulfill every desire, every passion, we might have. But wise men know that kind of "freedom" is actually slavery. We must value dignity, faithfulness, and honor over comfort, convenience, and self-centeredness. And—most critically—we must ensure that the freedom to do what we should remains exactly what it is: a choice. None of this can be mandated. It defeats the entire purpose.

Equally important, relationships matter. Yes, "we" has its place. Humans were made for communion.

This is why we as individuals find our most profound meaning in connection with others. In coming together to form something bigger than ourselves. We were literally built for it. Anyone alive can tell you that. We feel it in our bones.

So, how to embrace that side of ourselves without devolving into various forms of collectivism? Without snuffing out the individual human spirit and its natural state of sovereignty?

The answer, I believe, lies in what makes us sovereign in the first place. Who are we? Why are we endowed with certain unalienable rights? What part of us is made in our Creator's image? What does all of this even mean? What does it matter?

So, if you'll indulge me here, I'd like to conclude by imparting a different kind of wisdom. Not my own, but rather, wisdom that has been passed down for thousands of years by the Orthodox Church—the oldest Christian church in the world, founded by Jesus Christ, and in which all other churches and groups can trace their origin.[168]

Despite the roughly 250 million Orthodox Christians worldwide, Orthodoxy is often misunderstood in the West, particularly for its simultaneous embrace of reason and mystery. Why mystery? For starters, once we acknowledge we aren't God, we recognize that our faith—the Faith—will always lie far beyond our full grasp. The truth is so big that, no matter how much we learn, we'll never fully grasp it. It is a treasure that cannot be exhausted. Additionally, while reason and knowledge are important and good, not everything is for us to know now. Learning this lesson is important for us but sometimes frustrating because we are prideful human beings.

Orthodox Christianity provokes us to think about the rhythm of life, the process, the journey. The ever-growing journey of knowing God and having an intimate experiential relationship with Him. Yet even with this direct, personal relationship, Orthodoxy recognizes that it is not simply about the individual. Orthodoxy is communal. Here, "we" finally has its place. Orthodoxy acknowledges that humans are made for communion and that our growth is dependent on this ability for communion, while we also grow to be more like Him who knows Himself as persons in communion—Father, Son, and Holy Spirit.

This collective, communal nature of the Church is critical. We are not saved alone but in a community. We need our brethren in order to be fully Christian. The hard work of communion is what creates the character of Christ within us and cultivates gratitude.

Created in the image of God, we humans are—and are meant to be—persons in communion. This image of God is in the very nature of the soul. We share in God's spiritual attributes and are made to become more Godlike, which includes immortality, freedom of will, reason, pure love, dominion in the world through service and kindness, and everlasting life in communion with God and creation.

There is a distinction between the image and the likeness of God, with the likeness being in the moral perfecting of man in virtue and sanctity, and in the acquirement of the gifts of the Holy Spirit. We receive the image of God from God Himself at the moment we begin to exist, but the likeness we must acquire ourselves, having received this ability from God. This is an eternal journey, but it includes our time here on Earth, and it's why our time on Earth is so important.

Fortunately, everything in the Church is meant to enable us to become like Him. It is within this unity of the

Church that man is what he is created to be and can grow for eternity in divine life that is in communion with God through Christ in the Holy Spirit. While it can begin for you today, this unity of the Church isn't broken by time or space, and it isn't limited merely to those alive today. It is the unity of the Trinity and *all* who live with God.

The Orthodox Church

The word *church* simply means those called as a particular people to perform a particular task. And the word *Orthodox* comes from the Greek, meaning correct worship, right worship, right belief, or most importantly, right glory. In understanding the Orthodox Church, it's helpful to understand how the Church sees herself. The Church knows herself as one (not denominated; just as Christ is one, so is His church), holy (set apart for a specific use), catholic (healthy, full, complete, mature, and universal; from the Greek word *katholikos* whose definition is too great to fully translate), and apostolic (the inheritors of the teachings of the apostles, committed and preserved without change).

If you haven't already, I invite you to submit yourself to a relationship with Jesus Christ as your soul seeks its restoration to health, wholeness, and well-being. This is the full meaning of the Greek word for *salvation*, and it's why it is a continuous process. Once we understand that the image of God is the very nature of the soul, it's easy to understand why our souls long for salvation, for this continuous restoration to health, wholeness, and well-being.

If you've ever thought to yourself, *There must be more*, may this be the beginning of your journey.

IN CLOSING | TRUTH

What is truth?

It's one of the most important questions we as humans can answer, and on its deepest level, it should lead us to eternal life and salvation. It should lead us to Christ, as He is Truth incarnate.

Understanding the created things discussed in this book must ultimately lead us beyond them to the far deeper truth of the *uncreated* Christ, the incarnate Logos. Truth is a person! The truth of Jesus Christ is no mere mental exercise, as even those on the side of darkness understand and acknowledge who He is. Rationally understanding truth isn't enough. The salvific (leading to salvation) eternal truth of Jesus Christ comes through a relationship with Him. And that experiential relationship is about our heart far more than it is about our head. When we have communion with Truth as a person, we're already enjoying the first fruits of eternal life. What a blessing.

The secular politicized collective never has and never will work. It's not ours to have. The collective belongs to God.

Fortunately, every time mankind foregoes the secular politicized collective and honors the sovereignty of the individual made in our Creator's image, we achieve new heights that once existed only in our dreams.

I'll say it again: Through our God-given reason and intellect, we're meant to grapple with the truth and revelation of all created things; therefore, it's essential that we understand all parts of our society, including politics, money, and the ideas that drive them. We may not be of this world, but we are here in it, and the decisions we make—and the actions we take—matter.

We exercise our rights in the secular world to reflect our love for our brethren. With our gaze ever fixed on the eternal, we know it is never to "win" or to control others. Exercising our rights and reclaiming liberty—even on behalf of those who disagree with us—is a privilege and an honor. We do so to restrain evil and to stand for truth.

Will you stand with us?

It can be a bit daunting to stand up in a world telling you to sit down. At times, reclaiming our liberty might even feel like a herculean task—like a moonshot at best. But here's the thing about moonshots: We went to the moon.

ACKNOWLEDGMENTS

This book wouldn't exist without the extraordinary support, love, and wisdom of so many people.

First and foremost, to my husband, Naveen—my partner in everything and a source of constant joy, unwavering love, and support. You gave me the incredible gift of time, allowing me to immerse myself fully in this journey. For that and so much more, I am endlessly grateful.

To my brother, Peter—my best friend. You make me laugh, you make me better, and you've read more drafts of this book than anyone should ever be subjected to. Yet you never hesitated to dive back in, offering your honest and thoughtful feedback every time. Your opinion means the world to me, and I will always look up to you, my big brother.

To Dad—you instilled in me a boundless curiosity, a love of life, and resilience that made this book—and all my crazy dreams—possible. You and Mom always believed in me, no matter how unconventional my path.

Mom fell asleep in the Lord in December 2023 after a horrific battle with Parkinson's, and not a day goes by that I don't miss her. While she never got to read this book, I like to think she would have rather liked it. It's Mom whom I can thank for my lifelong love of literature and learning.

To Stacie, George, Shirin, Saddad, Piya, Karina, Cyrah, Zara, Ayana, and our entire family—you bring a smile to each day, and your presence in my life is always a source of strength and inspiration.

To my brilliant editor, Jill Smith—your insights, patience, and vision elevated this book to heights I couldn't have reached on my own. Working with you has been an absolute privilege.

To the teams at Forefront Books and Simon & Schuster—your expertise and dedication brought this project to life in ways I never imagined. I'm endlessly thankful for your hard work and commitment.

And to Bruce Gore—your artistry captured the essence of this book perfectly. Thank you for giving it such a striking visual identity.

Finally, to the countless friends, colleagues, and readers who supported me along the way, whether with a kind word, an encouraging message, or a shared insight—you are all part of this story.

With deepest gratitude,
Chris

NOTES

1. Cybersecurity and Infrastructure Security Agency, "MDM Incident Response Guide," https://www.cisa .gov/sites/default/files/publications/mdm-incident -response-guide_508.pdf; U.S. Department of Homeland Security, "National Terrorism Advisory System," https:// www.dhs.gov/publications-library/national-terrorism -advisory-system#:~:text=The%20United%20States%20 remains%20in%20a%20heightened%20threat%20 environment%20fueled,foreign%20and%20domestic%20 threat%20actors; U.S. Department of Homeland Security, "National Terrorism Advisory System Bulletin: February 7, - Translations," https://www.dhs.gov/publication/national -terrorism-advisory-system-bulletin-february-7-2022 -translations; Cybersecurity and Infrastructure Security Agency, "Foreign Influence Operations and Disinforma- tion," https://www.cisa.gov/topics/election-security/foreign -influence-operations-and-disinformation; and Founda- tion for Freedom Online, *FFO Flash Report*, March 2023, https://foundationforfreedomonline.com/wp-content /uploads/2023/03/FFO-FLASH-REPORT-REV.pdf.

2. The Westlaw dictionary explains that a *term of art* is "a word or phrase that has a special meaning in a particular context. Legal terms of art denote words or expressions that have through usage by legal professionals acquired a distinct legal meaning." See https://content.next.westlaw .com/practical-law/document/I03414f21280f11e698dc8 b09b4f043e0/Term-of-Art?viewType=FullText&transition Type=Default&contextData=(sc.Default)#:~:text=A%20 word%20or%20phrase%20that,acquired%20a%20 distinct%20legal%20meaning%22.

3. Thomas Paine, *The Rights of Man* (1791).

4. "Knowledge will forever govern ignorance: And a people who mean to be their own Governors, must arm themselves with the power which knowledge gives." James Madison. *Letters and Other Writings of James Madison: Fourth President of the United States*. Published by order of Congress, 1865. Vol. 3. This letter can be found in Volume 3, specifically in the collection of Madison's writings addressed to W. T. Barry.

5. Benedikt Franke, "Animal Instincts," *The Monocle Minute*, January 4, 2024, https://monocle.com/minute/2024/01/04/.

6. Note that this is radically different than Humanism, a school of thought that rejects the notion of divine intervention or revelation and emphasizes human reason, values, and ethics. Thus, the organizing of the world is in order to satisfy man's earthly needs only.

7. This is the basic difference between natural vs. vested rights. Vested rights are created by the local, state, or national government for our protection or well-being. But they are not naturally ours and, thus, can be changed any time the lawmakers feel like it.

8. William Pitt, speech to the House of Lords, January 20, 1770.

9. Ludwig von Mises, *Human Action: A Treatise on Economics* (Yale University Press, 1949), chap. 1, sec. 1, "Purposeful Action and Animal Reaction."

10. G. Michael Hopf, "Hard Times," *G. Michael Hopf*, accessed May 16, 2024, https://www.gmichaelhopf.com/hard-times. Hopf was influenced by the Strauss-Howe Generational Theory, advanced in their books, *Generations* and *The Fourth Turning*. Of course, the concept itself can be traced back to Plato and has been echoed by philosophers throughout the ages. Eighteenth-century Scottish historian Alexander Fraser Tytler, viewing the concept within a political context, gave us what's colloquially known as the "Tytler Cycle": From bondage to spiritual faith. From spiritual faith to great courage. From courage to liberty. From liberty to abundance. From abundance to selfishness. From selfishness to complacency. From complacency to apathy. From apathy to dependence. From dependence back again to bondage.

11. Gallup, Inc., "Church Attendance Has Declined Across Religious Groups," 2023, https://news.gallup.com/poll/642 548/church-attendance-declined-religious-groups.aspx.

12. Saifedean Ammous, *The Bitcoin Standard: The Decentralized Alternative to Central Banking*, updated ed. (Hoboken, NJ: Wiley, 2021), 22, 24. See also Gold.org for up-to-date information.

13. A "fixed exchange rate" occurs when one currency is tied or "fixed" to another so that the trade value remains stable and predictable. For example, if the colonists set a fixed exchange rate, 6 wampum shells might be equal to 1 English shilling. So, if you want to buy something worth 2 shillings, you

could pay 12 wampum shells instead of using metal coins. This allows both the colonists and Indigenous peoples to trade easily using a consistent value for both currencies.

14. "Jiaozi," *Wikipedia*, https://en.wikipedia.org/wiki/Jiaozi _(currency)#:~:text=Jiaozi%20(Chinese%3A%20%E4%B A%A4%E5%AD%90),(960%E2%80%931279%20CE).

15. Marco Polo, *The Travels of Marco Polo*, ed. Ronald Latham (New York: Penguin Books, 1958).

16. US President Franklin Delano Roosevelt had outlawed the private ownership of gold via Executive Order 6102 on April 5, 1933.

17. Shipwrecked sailor David O'Keefe was initially looking to profit off the island's coconuts and needed to encourage the Yapese to work for him. This ultimately turned into procuring the requisite technology from Hong Kong to quarry the Rai stones and use them as payment to the Yapese.

18. James Blanchard, "An Interview with F. A. Hayek" (interview by James Blanchard, May 1, 1984).

19. Ralph Merkle, "DAOs, Democracy, and Governance," *Cryonics* 37, no. 4 (July–August 2016): 28–40, https://www .cryonicsarchive.org/docs/cryonics-magazine-2016-04.pdf.

20. Thomas Jefferson, letter to Gideon Granger, 1800, in *The Papers of Thomas Jefferson, Memorial Edition*, vol. 10, ed. Paul Leicester Ford (Washington, DC: Thomas Jefferson Memorial Association, 1903), 168.

21. William Ebenstein and Alan Ebenstein, *Great Political Thinkers: Plato to the Present*, 6th ed. (Belmont, CA: Wadsworth Cengage Learning Publishing, 1999). See also W. Cleon Skousen, *The Five Thousand Year Leap: Twenty-Eight Great Ideas That Are Changing the World* (United States: National Center for Constitutional Studies, 1981).

22. W. Cleon Skousen, *The Five Thousand Year Leap: Twenty-Eight Great Ideas That Are Changing the World* (United States: National Center for Constitutional Studies, 1981), 39.

23. John Locke, "Second Essay Concerning Civil Government," in *Great Books of the Western World*, vol. 35, ed. Robert Maynard Hutchins (Chicago: Encyclopaedia Britannica, 1952), 5–146.

24. William V. Wells, *The Life of Samuel Adams* (Boston: Little, Brown and Company, 1865).

25. John R. Howe Jr., *The Changing Political Thought of John Adams* (Princeton: Princeton University Press, 1966).

26. Alexander Ward and Heidi Przybyla, "Trump Allies Prepare to Infuse 'Christian Nationalism' into Second Administration," *Politico*, February 20, 2024, https://www.politico.com/news/2024/02/20/donald-trump-allies-christian-nationalism-00142086.

27. Wade Miller, X post, April 10, 2024, https://twitter.com/WadeMiller_USMC/status/1761015125673222572.

28. Miller, X post, April 10, 2024.

29. W. Cleon Skousen, *The Five Thousand Year Leap: Twenty-Eight Great Ideas That Are Changing the World* (United States: National Center for Constitutional Studies, 1981), 76; quote taken from George B. De Hussar, Henry W. Littlefield, and Arthur W. Littlefield, eds., *Basic American Documents* (Ames, IA: Littlefield, Adams & Co., 1953), 76.

30. Library of Congress, "Northwest Ordinance (1787)," https://guides.loc.gov/northwest-ordinance.

31. Skousen, *The Five Thousand Year Leap*, 1981, 78.

32. Albert Henry Smyth, ed., *The Writings of Benjamin Franklin*, vol. 1 (New York: Macmillan, 1905). See also Skousen, *The Five Thousand Year Leap*, 1981, 78.

33. George Washington, "Farewell Address," accessed June 29, 2024, https://avalon.law.yale.edu/18th_century/washing.asp. It's worth noting that Washington issued his warning partly in response to the scene in France, where atheists had seized control of public sentiment.

34. Alexis de Tocqueville, *Democracy in America*, trans. George Lawrence, ed. J.P. Mayer (New York: Harper & Row, 1966).

35. James Madison, "Federalist No. 10," *The Federalist Papers*, accessed April 13, 2024, https://guides.loc.gov/federalist -papers/text-1-10#s-lg-box-wrapper-25493273.

36. These questions were taken from the original examination on file at the Smokey Valley Genealogical Society and Library in Salina, Kansas.

37. Jim Mattis and Bing West, *Call Sign Chaos: Learning to Lead* (New York: Random House, 2019).

38. Aristotle, *Metaphysics*, trans. Hugh Lawson-Tancred (London: Penguin Classics, 1998).

39. Ashlee Vance, "Elon Musk's Mission to Mars," *Wired*, October 21, 2012, https://www.wired.com/2012/10/ff-elon -musk-qa/.

40. Daniel Bell, "The nation-state is too big for the small problems and too small for the big problems," *Wikiquote*, last modified June 2024, https://en.wikiquote.org/w/index.php ?title=World_Federalism&oldid=3111389.

41. Alan Cranston, *The Sovereign Revolution*, ed. Kim Cranston (Stanford: Stanford University Press, 2004), 28.

42. And, when seen in the Middle Ages, this sovereignty was significantly limited compared to that which came before or after.

43. Volker Gerhardt, "On the Historical Significance of the Peace of Westphalia: Twelve Theses," in *1648—War and Peace in Europe*, ed. Klaus Bussmann and Heinz Schilling

(s.l.: s.n., 1999), 444. See also Daniel Philpott, *Revolutions in Sovereignty* (Princeton: Princeton University Press, 2001), 82. Philpott appears throughout this chapter, and his analysis of Westphalia as a revolution in sovereignty is generally insightful.

44. *Respublica Christiana* refers to the Western Christian political and social order in Europe during the Middle Ages, emphasizing a unified Western Christian community governed by both secular and ecclesiastical authorities.

45. It's important to note that Westphalia wasn't alone in enshrining the notion of sovereign states in modern international relations. The collapse of colonial empires after WWII—fueled by the Cold War and consummated through the 1960 United Nations ("UN") Declaration on colonial independence and ensuing secession of British and French colonies in Latin America, Africa, and Asia—was a similarly momentous change in the world order, cementing global sovereign statehood. Similar to Westphalia, the UN Declaration is best seen as the consolidation of a trend.

46. Leo Gross, "The Peace of Westphalia, 1648–1948," *American Journal of International Law* 42, no. 1 (1948): 20–41.

47. United States, *Declaration of Independence* (Washington, DC: National Archives and Records Administration, 1776).

48. France, *Constitution of October 4, 1958*, art. 3.

49. Note that international law clearly delineates that war crimes and other such serious international crimes fall outside the scope of immunity, ensuring that individuals can be held accountable for these deemed grave offenses.

50. *Charter of the United Nations and Statute of the International Court of Justice*, https://treaties.un.org/doc/publication/ctc/uncharter.pdf.

51. United Nations, "Charter of the United Nations," chap. X, art. 71 (San Francisco, 1945), https://www.un.org/en/about-us/un-charter/full-text.

52. Civil society refers to the aggregate of NGOs, NPOs, and other institutions, such as community groups, advocacy groups, professional associations, faith-based associations, and labor unions, that supposedly manifest the interests and will of citizens.

53. Alan Cranston, *The Sovereign Revolution*, ed. Kim Cranston (Stanford: Stanford University Press, 2004), 39.

54. ZeroHedge, "World's Busiest Political Year Ever," https://cms.zerohedge.com/s3/files/inline-images/busiest%20political%20year%20ever_4.jpg?itok=iY9Ha.

55. Koh Ewe, "The World's Biggest Elections Are Happening in 2024. Here's What You Need to Know," *Time*, December 28, 2023, https://time.com/6550920/world-elections-2024/.

56. The UN Summit of the Future did take place in September 2024, and the General Assembly adopted the Pact for the Future. The US voted yes and was a leader in ensuring its passage. Notably, only seven countries voted no, including Russia and Iran; fifteen countries abstained, including China, but remain otherwise subject to the language. Only Argentina chose to dissociate itself completely from the Pact for the Future, making it clear that it would not be considered a participant, avoiding even implied endorsement or obligations under the Pact, and emphasizing the subjugation of sovereign nations to external decisions by the UN that directly interfere with their freedom.

57. United Nations, "Summit of the Future," accessed June 26, 2024, https://www.un.org/en/summit-of-the-future.

58. United Nations, "Our Common Agenda: Policy Brief on the Emergency Platform," last modified May 2023, https://www.un.org/sites/un2.un.org/files/our-common-agenda-policy-brief-emergency-platform-en.pdf.

59. United Nations, "Pact for the Future: Zero Draft," last modified June 2023, https://www.un.org/sites/un2.un.org/files/sotf-co-facilitators-zero-draft_pact-for-the-future.pdf.

60. United Nations, "Pact for the Future."

61. United Nations, "Pact for the Future."

62. United Nations, "Our Common Agenda."

63. United Nations, "Our Common Agenda."

64. "Coalition of 22 State AGs Call on Biden to Reject Treaty Drastically Expanding WHO Authority," *American Greatness*, May 9, 2024, https://amgreatness.com/2024/05/09/coalition-of-22-state-ags-call-on-biden-to-reject-treaty-drastically-expanding-who-authority/.

65. "Globalists Suffer Big Upset in Geneva and WHO Chief Urges Aggressive Crackdown on Skeptics," *The Blaze*, May 9, 2024, https://www.theblaze.com/news/globalists-suffer-big-upset-in-geneva-and-who-chief-urges-aggressive-crackdown-on-skeptics.

66. United Nations, *Our Common Agenda: Policy Brief 2—Strengthening the International Response to Complex Global Shocks—An Emergency Platform* (New York: United Nations, May 2023).

67. European Commission, "Corporate Sustainability Due Diligence," accessed June 27, 2024, https://commission.europa.eu/business-economy-euro/doing-business-eu/corporate-sustainability-due-diligence_en#what-are-the-obligations-for-companies.

68. European Parliament, "P9_TA(2024)0329: European Parliament Resolution of 23 June 2024 on the Corporate Sustainability Due Diligence Directive," accessed June 27, 2024, https://www.europarl.europa.eu/doceo/document/TA-9 -2024-0329_EN.html.

69. United Nations, "Our Common Agenda: Policy Brief on the Emergency Platform," last modified May 2023, https:// www.un.org/sites/un2.un.org/files/our-common-agenda -policy-brief-emergency-platform-en.pdf.

70. United Nations, "Our Common Agenda."

71. United Nations, "Our Common Agenda."

72. Joint Committee on the Investigation of the Pearl Harbor Attack, *Investigation of the Pearl Harbor Attack*, 79th Congress, 2nd Session, 1946, 252–253.

73. Central Intelligence Agency, *The Origin and Evolution of the CIA*, https://www.cia.gov/resources/csi/static/Origin-and -Evolution.pdf.

74. The title of DCI transferred to the head of the CIA in 1947 and would continue to be used until 2004, when the Intelligence Reform and Terrorism Prevention Act of 2004 created the position of Director of National Intelligence (DNI), reducing the CIA DCI's authority over the entire intelligence community.

75. Central Intelligence Agency, *The Origin and Evolution of the CIA*.

76. From 1789 to 1947, the War Department was responsible for the administration and operation of the US Army. It managed military affairs, including the organization, supply, and training of the Army.

77. All versions of NSCID 1 have been declassified and are available at the National Archives and Records Administration,

Record Group 263 (CIA), NN3-263-91-004, box 4, HS/HC-500.

78. National intelligence was later further defined in NSCID3 in 1948 as "integrated departmental intelligence that covers the broad aspects of national policy and national security, is of concern to more than one Department or Agency, and transcends the exclusive competence of a single Department or Agency or the Military Establishment." This was considered the opposite of "departmental" intelligence, defined by the same NSCID as intelligence needed by a department or agency "to execute its mission and discharge its lawful responsibilities." See Central Intelligence Agency. *The Origin and Evolution of the CIA*.

79. Central Intelligence Agency. *The Origin and Evolution of the CIA*.

80. The word *opportunities* here is forward-looking and refers to the potential for the intelligence community to enhance national security by proactively identifying and addressing emerging threats, leveraging technological advancements, and improving intelligence capabilities to safeguard national interests. It aligns with the document's intent to evaluate whether the intelligence community was prepared not only to respond to immediate challenges but also to seize strategic opportunities for strengthening the nation's security posture in a rapidly changing global landscape.

81. Central Intelligence Agency. *The Origin and Evolution of the CIA*.

82. See the following: Stephen Kinzer, *All the Shah's Men: An American Coup and the Roots of Middle East Terror* (Hoboken, NJ: Wiley, 2003); Mark J. Gasiorowski, "The 1953 Coup D'état in Iran," *International Journal of Middle*

East Studies 19, no. 3 (1987): 261–286; Malcolm Byrne, *The CIA's Secret History of the Iran Coup, 1953* (Washington, DC: National Security Archive, 2000); Kermit Roosevelt, *Countercoup: The Struggle for the Control of Iran* (New York: McGraw-Hill, 1979); Ervand Abrahamian, *The Coup: 1953, the CIA, and the Roots of Modern U.S.-Iranian Relations* (New York: New Press, 2013); and David Talbot, *The Devil's Chessboard: Allen Dulles, the CIA, and the Rise of America's Secret Government* (New York: Harper, 2015).

83. Glenn Beck, "RFK Jr: America's Economic Collapse Will Bring a Revolution," episode 217 of *The Glenn Beck Podcast*, podcast audio, April 20, 2024, https://www.glennbeck.com/st/the_glenn_beck_podcast.

84. Google, for example, has a longstanding and multifaceted relationship with various government agencies. In the late 1990s when Larry Page and Sergey Brin were Ph.D. students at Stanford University, the Defense Advanced Research Projects Agency (DARPA) provided early funding through the Digital Libraries Initiative, which aimed to develop technologies for managing large digital libraries. In 2004, Google acquired a company called Keyhole Inc., which was founded in 2001 and specialized in developing Earth visualization tools. Keyhole's technology allowed users to zoom in and out of a 3D globe, providing a detailed and interactive view of the Earth. Keyhole's main product, Earth Viewer, was the precursor to Google Earth and Google Maps, and the acquisition provided Google with the foundational technology for its mapping services. Keyhole received funding from In-Q-Tel, the venture capital arm of the CIA. In-Q-Tel invests in companies that develop technologies of interest to US intelligence agencies.

85. Victoria Nuland, "Remarks at the U.S.-Ukraine Foundation Conference," U.S. Department of State, December 13, 2013, https://geneva.usmission.gov/2013/12/17/assistant-secretary -nuland-speaks-at-u-s-ukraine-foundation-conference/.

86. Office of Personnel Management, "Federal Workforce Data," accessed June 9, 2024, https://www.opm.gov/policy -data-oversight/data-analysis-documentation/federal -employment-reports/.

87. Chico Q. Camargo and Felix M. Simon, "Mis- and Disinformation Studies Are Too Big to Fail: Six Suggestions for the Field's Future," *Harvard Kennedy School (HKS) Misinformation Review*, September 20, 2022, https://misinforeview .hks.harvard.edu/article/mis-and-disinformation-studies -are-too-big-to-fail-six-suggestions-for-the-fields-future. See also https://doi.org/10.37016/mr-2020-106.

88. Joe Rogan, "Edward Snowden," *The Joe Rogan Experience*, episode 1368, October 23, 2019, Spotify, https://open .spotify.com/episode/3J0Rih8QZwaLI3AXwTQ4Oc.

89. Argentina's Milei on Dollarization, Central Bank," Bloomberg video, August 16, 2023, accessed June 28, 2024, https://www.bloomberg.com/news/videos/2023-08 -16/argentina-s-milei-on-dollarization-central-bank-video.

90. Tobias Käufer, "Argentina: Javier Milei's First 100 Days of Hope and Concern," *DW.com*, last modified March 18, 2024, accessed June 29, 2024, https://www.dw.com /en/argentina-javier-mileis-first-100-days-of-hope-and -concern/a-68606230.

91. Peter Johnson and Sai Nimmagadda, *BH Digital—Focus Note—The Relentless Rise of Stablecoins* (Coremont, August 25, 2023), PDF. See also: "Stablecoin Supply," *Visa Onchain Analytics Dashboard*, accessed June 28, 2024, https://visa onchainanalytics.com/supply.

92. "Financials," *Visa Annual Report*, Accessed June 28, 2024, https://annualreport.visa.com/financials/default.aspx.

93. "PayPal Statistics," *Business of Apps*, Accessed June 28, 2024, https://www.businessofapps.com/data/paypal-statistics/.

94. "ACH Network Moves 30 Billion Payments, $77 Trillion in 2022 Led by Growth in Same Day ACH and B2B," *Nacha*, accessed June 28, 2024, https://www.nacha.org/news/ach -network-moves-30-billion-payments-77-trillion-2022-led -growth-same-day-ach-and-b2b.

95. "Annual Statistics: Volume and Value," *Federal Reserve Financial Services*, accessed June 28, 2024, https://frb services.org/resources/financial-services/wires/volume -value-stats/annual-stats.html.

96. Visa, *Visa and Crypto.com Enable USDC Payments Across Businesses Worldwide: A Case Study*, https://usa.visa .com/content/dam/VCOM/regional/na/us/Solutions /documents/visa-crypto.com-usdc-case-study.pdf. Access was expanded to include Solana in 2023. For VISA's thoughts on Solana's potential here, see Mustafa Bedawala and Arjuna Wijeyekoon's article, "A Deep Dive on Solana, a High Performance Blockchain Network," *Visa Crypto Solutions*, https://usa.visa.com/solutions/crypto/deep-dive -on-solana.html.

97. "PayPal Launches U.S. Dollar Stablecoin." *PayPal Newsroom*, August 7, 2023. https://newsroom.paypal-corp .com/2023-08-07-PayPal-Launches-U-S-Dollar-Stablecoin.

98. "PayPal Launches," *PayPal Newsroom*. https://newsroom. paypal-corp.com/2023-09-20-PayPal-USD-is-now-available -on-Venmo.

99. Keep in mind that stablecoins, like bitcoin, are digitally native assets. As such, they will only ever exist as an entry on

the stablecoin network's ledger. What a person possesses are the rights to control the entries (and thus, sell or transfer control of the coins) pertaining to the amount of the stablecoin that you own. Traditional usage and transference language is used in this chapter for ease of reading and understanding.

100. "Transparency," *Tether*, https://tether.to/en/transparency /?tab=usdt.

101. "Transparency," *Tether*.

102. "Circle Internet Financial," *World Economic Forum*, https:// www.weforum.org/organizations/circle-internet-financial/.

103. Agustín Carstens, "Cross-Border Payments—A Vision for the Future," filmed October 14, 2020, at the IMF Annual Meetings, YouTube video, 59:53, accessed June 28, 2024, https:// www.youtube.com/watch?v=mVmKN4DSu3gCarstens.

104. Ruchir Agarwal and Signe Krogstrup, "Cashing In: How to Make Negative Interest Rates Work," *IMF Blog*, February 5, 2019, https://www.imf.org/en/Blogs/Articles/2019 /02/05/blog-cashing-in-how-to-make-negative-interest -rates-work.

105. *Connecting Economies through CBDC: BIS Innovation Hub Project mBridge*, Bank for International Settlements, October 2022, accessed June 28, 2024, https://www.bis.org /publ/othp59.pdf. Note that the US is now participating.

106. "CBDC Tracker," *CBDC Tracker*. Accessed June 28, 2024. https://cbdctracker.org/.

107. "Full Committee Hearing: The Semiannual Monetary Policy Report to the Congress," *United States Senate Committee on Banking, Housing, and Urban Affairs*, February 29, 2024, https://www.banking.senate.gov/hearings/02/29 /2024/the-semiannual-monetary-policy-report-to-the -congress.

108. "Jerome Powell's Testimony," YouTube video, 1:28:45, posted by "Federal Reserve," March 7, 2024, accessed June 28, 2024, https://www.youtube.com/watch?v=kz0o3NJQpX0.

109. Katie Camero, "Why Did CDC Change Its Definition for 'Vaccine'? Agency Explains Move as Skeptics Lurk," *Miami Herald*, September 27, 2021, https://www.miamiherald.com/news/coronavirus/article254111268.html.

110. The US Supreme Court, its decision in *Fischer v United States*, has shown the "insurrection" to be more of a legal case of mass trespass and unlawful entry. Supreme Court of the United States. *Petitioner v. Respondent*. No. 23-5572. June 29, 2023. https://www.supremecourt.gov/opinions/23pdf/23-5572_l6hn.pdf.

111. Democracies fail for the simple reason that a crisis can (and usually does) whip people into a frenzy, at which point they'll vote based on passion in the heat of the moment. Purely democratic systems exploit our reactionary nature, whereas a republic intentionally slows our processes such that reason might prevail. James Madison spoke eloquently about the critical distinctions between democracies and republics in Federalist No. 10; see: Madison, James, "Federalist No. 10," *The Federalist Papers*, accessed April 13, 2024, https://guides.loc.gov/federalist-papers/text-1-10#s-lg-box-wrapper-25493273https://guides.loc.gov/federalist-papers/text-1-10#s-lg-box-wrapper-25493273.

112. "New Socialist Society," *New York Times*, September 12, 1905. See also W. Cleon Skousen, *The Five Thousand Year Leap: Twenty-Eight Great Ideas That Are Changing the World* (United States: National Center for Constitutional Studies, 1981).

113. Wilson, Woodrow, "Address to Congress," April 2, 1917, https://www.ourdocuments.gov/doc.php?flash=false&doc=61&page=transcript.

114. U.S. War Department, *1928 U.S. Army Training Manual No. 2000-25*, Internet Archive, 90–91, https://archive.org/details/pdfy-X8kxTtso2nVVynxP/page/n1/mode/2up.

115. U.S. War Department, *1928 U.S. Army Training Manual*, 92.

116. W. Cleon Skousen, *The Five Thousand Year Leap: Twenty-Eight Great Ideas That Are Changing the World* (United States: National Center for Constitutional Studies, 1981), 159.

117. Michel Foucault, *The Archaeology of Knowledge*, translated by A. M. Sheridan Smith (New York: Pantheon Books, 1972).

118. Immanuel Kant, *Critique of Pure Reason*, translated by Norman Kemp Smith, 2nd ed. (New York: St. Martin's Press, 1965).

119. Albert G. Mackey, *The Symbolism of Freemasonry: Illustrating and Explaining Its Science and Philosophy, Its Legends, Myths and Symbols* (New York: Clark & Maynard, 1882).

120. Albert Pike, *Morals and Dogma of the Ancient and Accepted Scottish Rite of Freemasonry* (Charleston: Supreme Council, 1871).

121. Theosophy seeks to show the underlying unity of all religions and incorporates and combines elements of Eastern religions, like Hinduism and Buddhism, with Western esoteric traditions, such as Gnosticism and Kabbalah. As for Satanism, the universal spirituality ideology doesn't allow for exclusions, hence Satanism's equal treatment and public acceptance we see today.

122. Lucis Trust, "Support the UN," https://www.lucistrust.org/about_us/support_un.

123. Lucis Trust, "About Lucis Trust," https://www.lucistrust
     .org/about_us/lucis_trust.

124. Most of the following information was found at the Alice
     Bailey page at https://theosophy.wiki/en/Alice_Bailey and
     https://en.wikipedia.org/wiki/Alice_Bailey.

125. Lucis Trust, "About Alice A. Bailey," https://www.lucistrust
     .org/books/about_alice_a_bailey.

126. The word *orthodox* here means traditional and conservative.
     It is not connected to the Orthodox Church; Bailey was
     raised in the Anglican Church.

127. Lucis Trust, "About Alice A. Bailey."

128. George F. Kennan, "Foreign Affairs; Now a Word From X,"
     interview by Thomas L. Friedman, *The New York Times*, May 2,
     1998, https://www.nytimes.com/1998/05/02/opinion/foreign
     -affairs-now-a-word-from-x.html.

129. Robert M. Gates, *Duty: Memoirs of a Secretary at War* (New
     York: Alfred A. Knopf, 2014), 157.

130. World Economic Forum, "Centre for the Fourth Industrial
     Revolution,"   https://centres.weforum.org/centre-for-the
     -fourth-industrial-revolution/home.

131. U.S. Agency for International Development, *Ukraine: Eco-
     nomic Reform and Transformation* (2018), https://pdf.usaid
     .gov/pdf_docs/PNACQ263.pdf.

132. World Economic Forum, "World Economic Forum and
     Ukraine Agree to Work Towards Country's Digital Trans-
     formation," January 2024, https://www.weforum.org/press
     /2024/01/world-economic-forum-and-ukraine-agree-to
     -work-towards-country-s-digital-transformation. See also
     Diia City, accessed August 21, 2024, https://diia.gov.ua.

133. Daryna Kolomiiets, "Diia—Ukraine's Digital Success
     Story," *Kyiv Post*, December 31, 2021, https://www.kyivpost
     .com/post/6941.

134. Diia City, https://city.diia.gov.ua/.Diia City.

135. World Economic Forum, "Ukraine to Launch a Global Government Technology Centre in Kyiv," May 2024, https://www.weforum.org/press/2024/05/ukraine-to -launch-a-global-government-technology-centre-in-kyiv/.

136. U.S. Agency for International Development, "A U.S.-Supported E-Government App Accelerated the Digital Transformation of Ukraine; Now Ukraine is Working to Scale the Solution to More Countries," January 18, 2023, https://www.usaid.gov/news-information/press-releases /january-18-2023-us-supported-e-government-app -accelerated-digital-transformation-ukraine.

137. Ukrainian Business News, "Ukraine Will Receive Tens of Millions of Dollars Due to Other Countries' Launch of a Diia Analog," February 6, 2023, https://ubn.news/ukraine-will -receive-tens-of-millions-of-dollars-due-to-other-countries -launch-of-a-diia-analog.

138. Tucker Carlson, "The Vladimir Putin Interview," accessed August 21, 2024, https://tuckercarlson.com/the-vladimir -putin-interview.

139. Carlson, "The Vladimir Putin Interview," 1:08:07.

140. Carlson, "The Vladimir Putin Interview."

141. Carlson, "The Vladimir Putin Interview," 28:17. It's worth noting that on multiple occasions in this interview, Vladimir Putin described American presidents as being impotent to make foreign policy decisions and referenced their overrule by a bureaucratic State Department.

142. Charles Clover, *Black Wind, White Snow: The Rise of Russia's New Nationalism,,* (New Haven, Yale University Press, 2016), 152.

143. Clover, *Black Wind, White Snow,* 153.

144. Clover, *Black Wind, White Snow,* 154.

145. Clover, *Black Wind, White Snow*, 154. The song quoted speaks of *Sovdep*. Originally a White Russian epithet for the Bolshevik leadership, Sovdep was a derogatory term denoting those supportive of Soviet ideology, morals, and habits.

146. C.M. Woodhouse, *Gemistos Plethon: The Last of the Hellenes*, (Oxford, Clarendon Press, 1986), 168. See also Heiser, *Prisci Theological and the Hermetic Reformation in the 15th Century*, 17–18.

147. James Heiser, *The American Empire Should Be Destroyed: Alexander Dugin and the Perils of Immanentized Eschatology* (Malone, TX, Repristination Press, 2014), 18; referencing Heiser's *Prisci Theological and the Hermetic Reformation in the 15th Century*, 35–46.

148. Frances A. Yates, *Giordano Bruno and the Hermetic Tradition*, (Chicago, University of Chicago Press, 1964), 12–13.

149. Heiser, *The American Empire Should Be Destroyed*, 20.

150. Anastasia V. Mitrofanova, *The Politicization of Russian Orthodoxy: Actors and Ideas*, (Stuttgart: Ibidem-Verlag, 2005), 137. See also Heiser, *The American Empire Should Be Destroyed*, 28.

151. Halford J. Mackinder, *Democratic Ideals and Reality: A Study in the Politics of Reconstruction* (New York: Henry Holt and Company, 1919).

152. Patrushev, Nikolay. Interview by *Izvestiya*. May 2009. Accessed via *Centre for Defence Strategies*. 2023. https://www.stopfake.org/en/in-moscow-a-new-eurasianism/.

153. Alexander Dugin, *The Fourth Political Theory* (London: Arktos Media Ltd., 2012), Ebook, Chapter 1, "The Birth of the Concept."

154. Dugin, *Fourth Political Theory*, Chapter 1.

155. Dugin, *Fourth Political Theory*, Chapter 2, "Dasein as an Actor."

156. Dugin, *Fourth Political Theory*, Introduction, "To Be or Not to Be."

157. James Heiser, *The American Empire Should Be Destroyed: Alexander Dugin and the Perils of Immanentized Eschatology* (Malone, TX, Repristination Press, 2014), 20.

158. Anton Barbashin and Hannah Thoburn, "Putin's Brain: Alexander Dugin and the Philosophy Behind Putin's Invasion of Crimea," *Foreign Affairs*, March 31, 2014, https://www.foreignaffairs.com/articles/russia-fsu/2014-03-31/putins-brain.

159. Owen Matthews, "Putin's Rasputin: Meet Alexander Dugin, the Mystic Who Helped Wreck the World," *Newsweek*, July 30, 2017, https://www.newsweek.com/2017/08/11/alexander-dugin-putin-brain-rasputin-eurasianism-642284.html.

160. Alexander Dugin, *The Great Awakening vs the Great Reset* (London: Arktos Media, 2021), Ebook, Chapter 4, "The Great Awakening."

161. Dugin, *The Great Awakening*, Chapter 3, "The Schism in the U.S.: Trumpism and Its Enemies."

162. "Putin Signs Decree Granting Residency to Foreigners Who Share 'Traditional Russian Values.'" *The Moscow Times*, August 19, 2024. https://www.themoscowtimes.com/2024/08/19/putin-signs-decree-granting-residency-to-foreigners-who-share-traditional-russian-values-a86074.

163. Dugin, *The Great Awakening*, from Chapter 4, "Theoretical Principles of the Great Awakening (Based on the Fourth Political Theory)."

164. Dugin, *The Great Awakening*, from Appendix: "The Great Awakening: The Future Starts Now."

165. Snyder, Andrew, "X," January 20, 2024, https://x.com /Andrewnsnyder/status/1748802195569418649.

166. Wikipedia, "The Satanic Bible," *Wikipedia: The Free Encyclopedia*, last modified August 7, 2023, https://en.wikipedia .org/wiki/The_Satanic_Bible.

167. *The X-Files*, Season 10, Episode 6, "My Struggle II," directed by Chris Carter, aired February 22, 2016, on Fox.

168. Throughout this section, I've relied on Faith Encouraged TV (in particular, Faith Encouraged TV, "Orthodoxy 101 Boot Camp Session 1," *YouTube video*, 56:52, August 14, 2013. https://www.youtube.com/watch?v=Q wxmQtnub50&list=PLwxwrDvy107nMKBngf3T9wsg XfxRb6R1b&index=7.); Faith Encouraged Substack by Father Barnabas Powell (in particular, Barnabas Powell, "Our Commonwealth Is in Heaven," *Faith Encouraged*, June 26, 2023, https://faithencouraged.org/our -commonwealth-is-in-heaven/); The Orthodox Church in America (in particular, Alexander Schmemann, "Man," *The Orthodox Faith*, Orthodox Church in America, https:// www.oca.org/orthodoxy/the-orthodox-faith/doctrine -scripture/the-symbol-of-faith/man), and Saint Andrew Greek Orthodox Church Blog (in particular, Stanley S. Harakas, "The Image of God in Man," *Saint Andrew Greek Orthodox Church*, March 21, 2016, https://saintandrewgoc .org/blog/2016/3/21/the-image-of-god-in-ma).